ALMA¡ BRITISH GHOSTS

RUTH ROPER WYLDE

COVER PHOTO: *Scenery around Glen Coe, Scotland. See Chapter 2 Feb 13th.*

Prologue

Chapter 1 – January

Chapter 2 – February

Chapter 3 – March

Chapter 4 – April

Chapter 5 – May

Chapter 6 – June

Chapter 7 – July

Chapter 8 – August

Chapter 9 – September

Chapter 10 – October

Chapter 11 – November

Chapter 12 - December

Prologue

Welcome, everyone, to this my second book on ghosts. I hope you enjoy reading it as much as I have enjoyed writing it – even if at times I had to go and watch a few comedy programmes on T.V. before I could go to bed to stave off nightmares about ghosts!

At the risk of repeating myself, for those people who read the prologue to my first book, The Ghosts of Marston Vale, one of the most common questions I get asked when people find out what I'm doing with all my spare time now that I am partially retired is "Do you believe in ghosts then?" This is often quickly followed by "Have you seen a ghost?"

I don't find either of the questions a "quick" one to answer. So let me try to explain – but it is more logical to answer them the other way around..

Have I ever seen a ghost? Well – I don't know. I've **seen** quite a lot of really inexplicable things, and **experienced** even more over the years. But the point about "inexplicable" is exactly that – they are what they say on the tin. Inexplicable. As in, they don't fit into our rational, every day understanding of how the world works and how things should behave or move. But never has a ghostly figure drifted up to me and presented itself as a "ghost" – so I'm not sure what you would class what I have seen / experienced **as**.

Let me give just a couple of brief examples.

Growing up, we moved around a fair bit in our childhood due to my father's changing job roles. We lived in different parts of the country and therefore, obviously, different houses. In my young schoolchild years, we were living in a bungalow in Suffolk, which was built on the grounds of an old prison (the one where there very last public hanging in Britain took place - the hanging of the Red Barn Murderer).

I can vividly remember often, when I walked home from school alone (because my older sister was too cool to hang out with her nuisance of a younger sibling), I would comfort myself with the knowledge that "my dog" would be waiting for me under the trees of the driveway that led down past the other bungalows to ours.

"My dog" was a black and white Border Collie type dog – but curiously sometimes he looked a bit more like an Alsatian. He would be sitting waiting for me, then would quietly walk to my side and pace alongside me for the last little bit of my walk home. I would let my hand rest on his head, or if he was a bit bigger that day, on his back – and sometimes I could feel him and sometimes I couldn't. He always disappeared just before I entered our own garden. And I actually mean disappear – as in there one second, gone the next. I never actually saw him *do* the disappearing that I recall.

I never remember being bothered that he somehow wasn't quite real – I wasn't sure whether I was making him up or whether he was actually there – and to be honest, in that childlike acceptance of things, I didn't really care either way. I just liked his company.

We moved away after a few short years, and I would probably have grown up thinking of him as a childhood fantasy friend: apparently so many children make up imaginary friends don't they?

Except I vividly remember my sister (with whom I shared a bedroom) waking up one night in the middle of the night and screaming. She screamed because she said "there was an Alsatian-like dog sitting by the head of my bed watching me sleep" and it gave her a fright. I had never told her about my friend, as far as I remember.

The house we moved to after that one was very peculiar. I won't bore you with every single thing that happened there – because frankly that would make for a ridiculously long prologue and would probably be enough to be a book in its own right. Suffice to say that things would move by themselves. And I don't mean in the, "I put it down just there and now I can't find it" way. I mean in the "my Mum and I are standing here in broad daylight watching that tea towel fold itself neatly into a square and we're both gob smacked" sort of a way.

But one of the worst things it used to do was scare my poor sister into a blithering wreck whenever she was trying to have a bath. Our grandparents lived with us by this point in our lives, and they had what is now known as a "granny flat" at one end of the house. It was actually a little two bedroom dwelling in its own right – two storied and with its own front door, lounge, kitchen, and two bathrooms. There were adjoining doors between the two properties both upstairs and downstairs. Because my parents were busy renovating the bathroom in "our" end of the house, we all used the "upstairs" bathroom in "Nanna's" end of the house by traipsing through our parents' bedroom and through the adjoining door.

My sister (older than me, as you recall) became quite frightened about going and having a bath whenever Nanna and Grandad weren't home (they liked to travel a lot in their old camper van) because she said something would come and bang on the bathroom door.

Eventually, she nagged and pleaded so much I agreed to go with her and sit in the bathroom while she had her bath. Sure enough, as we were chatting away – me sat on the folded loo seat, she in the bath – an almighty pounding started on the bathroom door. And I mean a proper fist banging pounding – the door was rattling in its frame.

My sister start to speak and I instantly shushed her – I was convinced it was a family member trying to frighten her and they wouldn't know I was in there with her. How easy to give them a fright back! So I crept to the door (still being pounded on) and flung it open – expecting the embarrassed culprit to half fall into the room with the violence of their motion.

There was no-one there.

So – what was it? A poltergeist? Our imagination? I really don't know – because the whole point of these inexplicable things is as I said earlier – they seem inexplicable!

Either way, these and many other experiences started a lifelong fascination for me with all things that go bump in the night. And day time. Wherever you are and whatever the time. Things still go bump. So it's not, for me, a case in "believing" in them. They are there. I just don't know what they are. And that bugs the investigator in me endlessly.

So please read on – this book is solely about the ghosts or entities or whatever they are that are supposed to only haunt on one night of the year. I'm kind of hoping that by writing an Almanac of when and where to look for them – some of you might go and see for me if anything is there. And hopefully write to me and let me know what you found…

Happy ghost hunting x

Ruth Roper Wylde
25.11.2017

wa-1400@outlook.com

Chapter 1 – January

There seem to be quite a number of ghosts who ritually haunt in a specific month, rather than any specific actual date within the month, so I am starting each chapter with those stories for ease of reference. Date specific tales are listed under the relevant date.

Brimpton, Berkshire

Brimpton is a very small village to the east of Newbury and just south of the A4. The legend is that every January, there is a ghostly re-enactment of the tragedy that struck when all the passengers in a coach drawn by four horses were killed on their way to a Ball when it overturned on Brimpton Lane at Able Bridge during a storm – plunging into the icy waters which raged below. Legend says that you can hear the screams of the passengers and the terrified whinnying of the horses as they are swept to their deaths.

Maps today show Brimpton Lane as actually starting at Brimpton Common, a few mile further south than Brimpton itself. Able Bridge appears to be where the Brimpton Lane crosses over the River Enbourne between Brimpton Common and Brimpton.

I wasn't able to find any actual accounts of someone encountering the phenomena. I did find one source which said it was a hunt ball specifically – and that might mean that the most likely date is actually New Year's Day, since traditionally a lot of hunts were held on that day.

East Malling, Kent

East Malling in Kent lies just south of the M20 and not far to the west of Maidstone. Although quite built up now, it still lies close to more rural aspects, and once upon a time would have been quite a small village.

You might want to be a little careful driving around it at night though, especially if you get close to the location of Barming Woods, which lies between the charmingly named Sweets Lane and North Pole Road.

The ghost of a horseman riding at speed is seen darting around trees and across roads, and the last reported sighting I can find was in 1971. Apparently one witness described the entity charging towards their car, but then disappearing on impact. For some unknown reason the entity seems to prefer the month of January. There seems to be very little known about who he was or why he was haunting.

Gisborough Priory, North Yorkshire

Gisborough Priory is a ruined Augustinian Priory in North Yorkshire. It was one of the first Augustinian priories to be built in Britain, and was funded by the Bruce family, who were ancestors of Robert the Bruce. It is now managed by English Heritage and can be visited for free during its opening hours. The tale goes that on the first new moon of every year, whenever that happens to fall, the ghostly black monk makes his appearance, possibly protecting a buried horde of golden treasure.

It is difficult to find specific recent accounts of sightings, although apparently various mediums visiting the site at different times in the early 1990s all came away with the name of Edward, a monk who had been killed whilst sleeping.
In 2011 a paranormal investigation group visiting the site thought they saw a black figure seeming to approach the priory from the adjoining field, but fade in and out of view before fading altogether.

It seems likely therefore that this is still an active phenomena.

January 1st

The Hatches, Manningford Bruce, Wiltshire

The delightfully named Manningford Bruce is a small hamlet to the east of Devise in the picturesque countryside of rural Wiltshire, surrounded by rolling arable land and pleasant little coppices and woods. It was named after William de Breuse who held the manor in 1275. It was certainly occupied as far back as Roman times as there is the site of a Roman Villa near the church.

By the area known as The Hatches, each New Year's Day a Golden coach is said to pass through, pulled by four headless horses. There seems to be no story attached as to why this should be the case that I can find. However, the holder of the manor in 1086 was Grimbald the Goldsmith, and one can't help but wonder if the tale of a golden coach relates back to him in folk memory in some way.

There don't seem to be any actual records of sightings though, as far as I can determine.

High Hill House, Ferry Hill, County Durham – see also "Brass Farm 25th January"

In some accounts, this haunting is given as 1st January, but the more likely date is 25th January – for the full story go to that date.

Ilmington, Warwickshire

Ilmington is a very small village lying to the south of Stratford upon Avon in the Cotswolds, and boasts for itself the title of the highest village in Warwickshire, lying as it does at the foot of the Ilmington Downs.

It also has an embroidered map of all the old apple orchards in the village displayed in its church, as well as the fascinatingly pragmatic street names of Front Street, Middle Street and Back Street.

Every January 1st, so the saying goes, the ghost of a local Ilmington hunter goes hunting with his pack of hounds, and if he spies anyone and makes a request of them which they obey (such as opening a gate perhaps) then they will be carried off by him forever, having fallen under his diabolical spell.

The tale is supposed to be based on the life of a true resident of Ilmington, who became so obsessed by hunting that he let all else in his life fall to the wayside, including his attendance at church. One night he went out to his hounds because they were howling, but they did not recognise him and tore him to pieces.

The story however is reminiscent of many a cautionary tale for non-attendance at church, and bears tones of the Wild Hunt as well, an indelible part of European folklore.

Knighton Gorges Manor, Isle of Wight

Knighton Gorges Manor was in existence at least as early as 1202, but sadly was at least partially demolished in 1821 by its then owner George Maurice Bissett, allegedly in a fit of spite to stop his daughter from inheriting it, as he was angry with her for marrying beneath her station to a mere clergyman.

Despite its demise, local legend avers that it sometimes reappears in its former glory on either New Year's Day or New Year's Eve each year, or that the sound of merry making can be heard from the site by passers-by.

For further detail on the story, see New Year's Eve later in the book.

Overwater Hotel, Ireby, Cumbria.

Overwater Hotel is a stunning, white fronted building with four stately pillars at its entrance. Set in 18 acres of beautiful gardens this magnificent hotel is allegedly subject once a year to the visitation of a gruesome apparition.

Formerly an elegant country residence, Overwater Hall was purchased in 1814 by Joseph Gillbanks, who apparently embarked on an affair with a Jamaican girl.

When she inevitably fell pregnant to him, she then came to England and tracked him down. Rather than face the scandal he tried to drown her in nearby Overwater Tarn by taking her out on his boat and throwing her overboard. As the desperate girl tried to pull herself clear of the freeing waters, he mercilessly chopped her arms off so that she fell back and drowned.

Her sad, armless apparition is now said to visit the building once a year, and is said to announce her presence by knocking on the windows (quite a feat without arms..) Some versions of the tale suggest the date is actually New Year's Eve, not New Year's Day.

However, the true history of Joseph Gillbanks would seem to completely belie this lurid tale. Born in 1780 to a wealthy family, he sailed to Jamaica in 1800 to further his wealth.

There he met and married Mary, the niece of the Chief Justice of the Island. He returned to England with Mary as his wife in 1814, where he rebuilt Overwater Hall and made it the family seat.

He and Mary had three children, Jackson, Josephine and Mary.

His obituary in the Carlisle Patriot 12.02.1853 described him as

"His heartiness of manner and real kindness of disposition rendered him a great favourite. Mr. Gillbanks made no pretentions to polish; he prided himself on plain speaking, yet he had in his heart feelings which are much more valuable than mere ornament."

That doesn't sound much like someone who would callously cut the arms off a pregnant woman whilst trying to drown her.

A previous owner of the property, Mr De Courcy Barry wrote a regular column for "horse and Hounds" magazine for some fifty years, and he mentioned seeing the ghost gliding up the stairs and into the master bedroom. Interestingly, he saw the ghost in August, not January, and he also described her as someone who had been murdered by her husband, not her lover.

Curiously I came across other stories whilst researching this book of lovers who had been brought back to England from the plantations in America and then murdered by their supposed spouse once back on English soil, where their presence would no doubt be seen as an embarrassment in polite society.

Arthur's Stone, Reynoldston, South Glamorgan, Scotland

This next entry is not actually a haunting, but I thought it would be an interesting inclusion nevertheless.

Arthur's Stone, also known as Maen Ceti, is a Neolithic burial chamber, located on Cefyn Bryn common near Reynoldston, which can be visited free of charge but might need robust footwear as the tracks can be muddy.

Its capstone is a massive 25 ton quartz conglomerate boulder, which apparently was much larger prior to 1693 – when something unknown happened which split nearly a 10 ton chunk off its original mass.

Despite its massive bulk, apparently once a year on New Year's Day the stone walks itself down to a nearby stream to quench its thirst. Quite why, or who has actually seen evidence that it does this, does not seem to be known.

January 5th

Tainfield House, Kingston St Mary, Somerset

This is a very interesting little legend when you start to try and pin it down. Most references I can find about it say something along the lines of: Squire Surtees (who lived in the mid 1700's) rides a mottled grey horse and circles the driveway of Tainfield House, Kingston St Mary, rattling a handful of chains.

Most of the accounts I have read suggests he likes to do this on the 5th January, but I have seen one entry which suggests it was actually New Year's Eve. I have also found one reference where it is the main street of Kingston St Mary that he rides down, rather than by the house.

I haven't seen any mentions of this tale where it explains *why* exactly he rides like this.

And this is where it started to get a bit interesting. You see, I like to look up the history of the house, or of the individual, and see if from that I can piece together what is supposedly behind the haunting. In this case, at first I struggled to even find a reference to Tainfield House in Kingston St Mary. I found a map reference to Tainfield Cottages – and that suggested there may well have been a Tainfield House.

I wrote to the History Society at Kingston St Mary to ask them if they could shed any light, but in the meantime, I found a Squire Edward Surtees, who lived at Tanfield House, in Tanfield, West Yorkshire, in 1841 (the property is now a stunning events venue on the banks of the River Ure).

Since the entries in other references to the ghost books which gave a date just said "mid eighteenth century" (which would be mid 1700's) I began to wonder if the date 1841 doesn't get mis-translated as mid-18th century, and Tanfield House as Tainfield....

However, I very swiftly got a response from Ray and Alan (to whom my thanks!) at Kingston St Mary. It seems Tainfield House was built in 1810 next to an ancient farmhouse by a gentleman called Lt-General Richard Chapman.

It was described in 1813, shortly after Richard's death, as a newly built villa with 86 acres, comprising a dining room and drawing room, parlour and library, and with six bedrooms and a large stone balcony. The house remained in the Chapman family until 1944 when it was sold, and then divided into a number of separate dwellings which are still there on the southern edge of the village.

After Richard Chapman died, his widow continued to live in the house until her own death, and was joined in her later life by their eldest son Major-General Stephen Chapman and his wife. Stephen died in 1851, leaving Tainfield in the hands of his wife Caroline, who left it to go and live with family in Suffolk for a time.

Caroline then married William Edward Surtees in 1853, who came from a family with extensive property in the North East of England – and is conceivably perhaps therefore related to the Squire Edward Surtees who lived in Tanfield, West Yorkshire. It would seem probable, nevertheless, that actually the similarity in names for the two properties and the later family link is probably just a strange coincidence.

Although the married couple Caroline and Edward did not live at Tainfield for the first part of their marriage, and it was likely often left with a caretaker, it seems they did take up residence there from around the mid 1860's as William became a Somerset magistrate in 1860 and was regularly seen on the bench there after 1866.

In 1868 he purchased another property in the area and changed its name to the Manor House: and this probably earned him the nickname of "Squire" Surtees.

He was heavily involved in village life and seems to have been quite generous with his time and money, but his step family wrote of him as being "miserly". There is nothing however to shed light as to why he should be haunting the place on this particular date and rattling chains as he does so.

The Kingston St Mary History Society did however send me two recollections of ghosts which haunted the actual house before it was divided which make for interesting reading.

Apparently the villagers did not like to go near to Tainfield after dark, and one former resident wrote, "*The North Wing far bedroom was most definitely haunted and after my grandmother died…..this bedroom was even more avoided than before. We always thought it was a double haunting; my grandmother and someone else who was never identified. The whole house and grounds was [sic] always uncanny*".

The second account tells of how the gardener said that the area of the grounds known as "Church Walk" was haunted by a male ghost, whose identity was unknown. There was also a very ancient tree on the edge of the rose gardens, which the family's two dogs, an Alsatian and a terrier, used to react quite badly to.

Perhaps dividing the property finally put a closure to its paranormal activity.

January 6th

Hall'i'the'Wood Manor, Bolton, Lancashire

Hall'i'the'Wood Manor is an early 16th Century Manor House in Bolton, Lancashire. Currently, it serves as a museum, open two days a week with free entry. It is a stunning looking black-and-white half-timbered building (a popular style in English historical buildings of black beams with white plaster between in an intricate pattern), and was originally the home of a wealthy woollen merchant, and also the place where the Spinning Mule was invented for the weaving industry.

On January 6th, which is the date Christmas day used to fall on before the calendars were changed, it is said that the sound of rushing footsteps can be heard on the main staircase. There does not seem to be any associated tale of why the steps are heard.

The house is also reported to have two male ghosts, one dressed in black and one dressed in green, and the ghost of an old lady called Betty who shouts at children entering the property, telling them to get out.

Whitby Abbey, Yorkshire

This is another haunting which might be related to the fact that prior to the changing of the calendars, what is now 6th January used to be Christmas day.

Whitby Abbey today is a ruined St Benedictine Abbey overlooking the sea on the cliffs by Whitby in North Yorkshire – a picturesque and haunting setting if ever there was one. It is currently in the care of English Heritage, and is open to the public. There are numerous ghosts associated with the Abbey and its surrounds, and it was also part of the scenery which inspired Bram Stoker when writing "Dracula".

One ghost is that of a poor young nun, who fell in love when she shouldn't have, and was allegedly walled up alive near the main staircase, where she screamed relentlessly begging for forgiveness and her freedom until death overtook her. She allegedly still screams today by the staircase.

Supposedly, on 6th January if you stand quiet and still, you can hear the sounds of the monks chanting and singing from long ago…

January 11th

Green Park, London

Green Park in London lies between Hyde Park and St James Park, and covers around 47 acres of land – which is an impressively sized plot for the very centre of London. It forms a wonderful green oasis and haven of quiet amidst the city's bustle for shoppers, tourists, workers and residents alike – unless of course you happen to visit on January 11th. Legend says that on that night, you can hear the sound of heavy breathing and swords clashing.

The most commonly given explanation is that the spectral sound is related to a duel which was fought between Sir Henry Dutton Colt and the womaniser Robert Fielding, on January 11th 1696. The duel is said to have taken place close to where Cleveland Row backs onto the park. Although Robert wounded Sir Henry by running him through before he had time to draw his sword (no doubt considered an ungentlemanly thing to do) neither man died, and the fight ended when Sir Henry, the Baronet, disarmed Robert Fielding.

It seems strange that this incident should have caused a haunting, since neither protagonist died!

The park also has a tree in it apparently known as "the Tree of Death" for all the hangings that took place from its branches. It is said that birds and animals will not approach it, and that sometimes the wraith of a tall dark figure is seen near it, or low chuckling heard in its vicinity.

January 14th

West Deeping, Lincolnshire

West Deeping is a very small village in Lincolnshire, situated to the east of Stamford. It sits in a cluster of small villages with similar names, called "The Deepings", which sounds to me reminiscent of something Tolkien might write.

Parts of the village's Church of St Andrews were built in the 13th Century, and it is here that a ghost is said to haunt.
The story is that the sound of a woman's sobs can be heard on the anniversary of her death at 1am in the morning.

Elsewhere I have seen it listed that it is actually her husband you can hear sobbing, who, so distraught at losing his beloved wife, committed suicide the very next day – and his ghost haunts every January 15th.

January 15th

Tallington, Lincolnshire

Legend says that the husband of the lady who died in West Deeping on 14th January, inconsolable at the loss of his love, flung himself to his death from the bridge over the railway line at nearby Tallington, where he met his demise in the form of the London bound express train. Once a year, his ghostly form can be seen re-enacting his final moments at 5.50pm.

The slight snag with these two stories is that the railway crossing at Tallington is a level crossing – there is no proper bridge, only a narrow footbridge which looks quite difficult to fling oneself from, although not of course impossible. There also doesn't seem to be any record of anyone ever doing so at least as far back as 1803…

January 17th

Featherstone Castle, near Haltwhistle, Northumberland

Featherstone Castle began as a tower built in the mid-1300s by the Featherstonehaugh family, who held onto the property and expanded on it for some 400 years.

The tale of the ghosts of Featherstone Castle is a terribly sad one. Legend has it that at some time in the Medieval period, the then Baron of the castle (one of the Featherstonehaugh's – but different versions of the story give different times and names) decided to marry his daughter off in an appropriate match to further the fortunes and social standing of the family – but it was to a man she did not love as she already loved another.

The daughter tried to persuade her father otherwise and to put the marriage off, but inevitably the day of the wedding came.

Allegedly the bridal party rode out into the woods near Pinkyn Cleugh to hunt, but were ambushed by the lady's lover and his men, who hoped to steal her away. Unfortunately, the wedding guests and the Baron's men fought back, and the ensuing battle was ferocious and fought to the death on both sides.

At one point, the new husband lunged at the lover, but his bride flung herself between them to protect the man she loved, and received a mortal blow. Her lover then took his own life as he held the body of his beloved in his arms.

That night the Baron learned of the loss of his daughter and her retinue when their ghosts silently filed into the hall to take their places at the wedding banquet.

It is said that on the anniversary of the wedding every year, the wedding party can be seen either riding from Pinkyn Cleugh back towards the castle, or else in the Banquet hall holding the wedding feast that never took place in reality.

It seems quite feasible that the origin of the tale is an actual murder which took place on 24th October 1530 when Nicolas Fetherstonhaugh was murdered by William Ridley of Unthank and Hugh Ridley of Howden, possibly during a hunting party. The murder inspired Sir Walter Scott to write "The Death of Featherstonehaugh"

Today the castle is privately owned, but is hired out for some events. I cannot find where Pinkyn Cleugh might have been, but there is a nearby business called Yont the Cleugh Caravan Park which possibly sheds light on which direction the bridal party might have been coming from. However, "Cleugh" is a Gaelic word for a narrow valley so it might not necessarily be the same "cleugh".

As an aside, one of the nearby roads is called "Clattering Causeway" which is a fascinating name in its own right.

Interestingly, one of the Battles of the War of Rough Wooing, when Henry VIII sought to secure his northern borders by forcing a marriage between his son Edward and Mary Queen of Scots, was fought on 10th September 1547 at a place called Pinkie Cleugh just south of Edinburgh, in between Cousland and Dalkeith. One can't help but wonder if either the tales have twisted over time, or we have lost a meaning for the word Pinkyn or Pinkie – it might mean valley of the "[lost word]" and therefore like many place names is common in different areas .

January 19th

Biggin Hill Airfield, Near Bromley, Kent

Biggin Hill Airport still exists Near Bromley in Kent, and is a thriving busy little airfield close to the nation's capital. However, in the days of World War II it was RAF Biggin Hill, and was the main base for fighter planes protecting the capital and the country.

Known as "the Strongest Link", its fighters brought down 1,400 enemy aircraft, at the cost of 453 lives of personnel stationed at the base. A small part of the modern day airport still retains the moniker of RAF Biggin Hill.

For some reason, the distinctive sound of a Spitfire fighter plane is said to be heard every January 19th in the skies above the base. Some versions of the story claim that it can be seen, and performs a victory roll before mysteriously disappearing.

The local newspaper reported the story in 2008, and it mentioned that some people say the plane is actually a Merlin – but I think that might be some confusion since it is the engine in some of the Spitfire models that is called a Rolls Royce Merlin. I am sure someone who knows more about aviation history will be able to set us straight on that point.

One witness wrote in 2003 that he had heard it when it was actually snowing quite hard, and no old vintage plane could possibly have been flying that day.

I have been unable to find what the significance of the date in January is.

There are also numerous reports of the ghosts of airmen seen around the base, in the lanes and roads in the vicinity – and even inside houses which have been built over parts of what was the base originally.

There are reports from 1958, 1978 and 2011 of apparitions of airmen seen at the side of the road or crossing it near the base – so it would seem that the site remains very active.

Braddock Down, Lostwithiel, Cornwall

During the First English Civil War, a battle was recorded as fought on Braddock Down, near Lostwithiel in Cornwall, between the Parliamentarians and the Royalists, led by Sir Ralph Hopton, on 25th January 1643.

There was quite a large cavalry presence on the Parliamentarian force, but the battle was quite decisively won by the Royalists, and Sir Hopton gained accolade for how mercifully he treated his captured foes. Surprisingly, only a few hundred lives were lost, but well over a thousand men were taken prisoner.

Today, it is not known where, exactly, the Battle of Braddock Down took place. English Heritage believe it to be within parkland at Boconnoc. Since Braddock and Boconnoc are less than a mile and a half apart as the crow flies, one could reasonably safely assume the fighting took place "around that area" in terms of the ghostly presence supposed to manifest every anniversary of the battle.

Today, the area is still quite isolated and mainly wooded, so if you do happen to be walking or riding through there on January 25th, listen out for the inexplicable sound of thundering hooves, as if a large body of mounted cavalry were passing close by…

January 20th

Moons Moat, Redditch, Warwickshire

With such a romantic sounding name, it seems only fitting that the remains of this moated homestead or hunting lodge should boast a ghost.

Moons Moat was originally built in the thirteenth century but was extensively remodeled in the sixteenth century and although originally a homestead it was later extended to include fishing ponds and the moat – probably as a symbol of wealth and status. It was abandoned in the 17th century and is now a scheduled ancient monument, but is surrounded by a modern housing estate.

It is reportedly haunted by the ghost of Lady Mahun, who is seen every St Agnes Eve – 20th January. The Mahun's were the family who owned the property, and St Agnes' was the patron saint of virgins, in whose honour a feast would be held on 21st January.

The legend says she was either murdered or committed suicide – but there seems to be no record of either of these events for any of the historical figures bearing the title Lady Mahun, and frankly that does seem an unusually vague legend – there being quite a significant difference between having one's life stolen away and choosing to end one's own life.

Either event could conceivably lead to a haunting – but there seems little to link the story to the Mahun family, other than the fact that the ghost is supposedly wearing medieval clothing and is seen at what used to be a property belonging to them.

There was also a medieval "highway" in the area called "The Hollow Way" which was used by travellers for several hundred years – and of course that would have meant footpads, vagabonds and thieves would frequent it too.

January 25th

Nether Lypiatt Manor, Stroud, Gloucestershire

Nether Lypiatt Manor House is a small but perfectly formed manor house in Thrupp, near Stroud in Gloucestershire. It supposedly derives its name from a "leapgate" – a low gate which deer or horses could jump over but which would keep sheep and cattle contained. It was built in around 1702 by an unknown architect, commissioned by Judge John Coxe (or possibly his son, depending on which source you read). It became a little more well-known after 1980, when it was bought and lived in by Prince and Princess Michael of Kent. The Royal couple sold it in 2006.

It is also known for its ghostly blacksmith, who allegedly returns once a year and opens the gates to the Manor on the anniversary of his execution.

There are various versions of the story – the most common one seeming to be that a local blacksmith was found guilty of a crime (some of the versions say it was the crime of murder) and sentenced to hang, but Judge Coxe offered him a reprieve if he made new wrought iron gates for the manor house and they were found to be perfect in every possible way.

The blacksmith laboured away and produced a spectacular pair of gates, but the Judge claimed to find one small piece of wrought ironwork which was not quite symmetrical to its counterpart on the other gate, and so the hapless blacksmith was executed anyway. Once a year, the blacksmith's ghost returns and opens the gates that signaled his demise.

At some point not long before the 1980's, one of the owners of the house is said to have waited until midnight of the appointed day, and then slowly opened the gates to the astonishment of the waiting crowd of ghost hunters by means of a long piece of high tensile fishing line…

Another version of the tale states that once a year the body of the blacksmith returns carried by a great white horse, and having paraded round the courtyard of the manor, it disappears along with its forlorn burden.

Yet a third version claims that both these things happen: the gates open, the horse parades through with its burden – and also there is a great wailing cacophony from the trees around the house.

There is also supposed to be the spirit of a lady in grey haunting the house itself, as well as the ghost of the son of John Coxe, who allegedly hung himself in one of the bedrooms in the Manor. His unhappy ghost is said to have disturbed many of the owners with his wailing at night around the rooms of the house.

Brass Farm, County Durham – see also 1st January

The tale that is usually found relating to either 1st January or 25th January says that the murderer, Andrew, went on a killing spree at Brass Farm in County Durham, and his wild cries can still be heard at the farm on the date of the murders.
T
oday, High Hill Farm stands close to, or on the spot where, Brass Farm used to stand.

In 1682, the farm owners, John and Margaret Brass, were out at a party. During the evening, their servant boy Andrew Mills attacked and killed the three children who were left at home – their eldest daughter aged 20, their son aged 17, and their youngest daughter aged just 10.

He fled the scene but was either apprehended and was dragged, or took it upon himself to go, to the party where John and Margaret were celebrating.

According to a contemporary news report, he at first claimed that everyone at home had been murdered by a group of men who had broken in saying "kill them all!" Margaret took one look at his bloodstained clothes and his wild demeanour and called him a liar – saying it was Andrew himself who had killed her children. He then confessed, but claimed he had been made to do it by an evil entity he encountered in the house.

He was eventually convicted and sentenced to death. He was suspended in a metal cage, with his limbs bound, from the gibbet which stood near what is now the A167 between Ferry Hill and Thinford, and which has become known as Andrew's Stob. He would have died a slow and cruel death, and it is said his howls can still be heard along that stretch of road.

January 31st

Huddington Court, Huddington, Worcestershire

Huddington Court is a beautiful Grade I listed moated Manor House and is a private residence not open to the public.
It unwittingly secured a place in history as the home of one of the conspirators of the Gunpowder Plot which has result in our festivities these days on 5th November each year.

Sir Robert Wintour was the elder of the two brothers and the husband of Gertrude Wintour (nee Talbot). Thomas was the younger brother by three years. They were both embroiled in the Gunpowder Plot, and when Guy Fawkes was captured, they and other members of the group fled to Huddington Court initially.

It is said they arrived there around 2pm on 6th November 1605, where they took food, rest, and had a mass said for them, before fleeing again in the wee small hours of November 7th.

Several of the conspirators tried to drum up support locally, but it became quickly apparent that their cause was waning and would not succeed. The younger brother Thomas and some of his co-conspirators then holed up at nearby Holbeche House and when the soldiers came for them, tried to go down in a blaze of glory. Some died, but Thomas was captured and sent back to London where he was tortured.

Much of our historical knowledge of the Gunpowder Plot comes from the records of his confessions under torture, and he asked that he be hanged on behalf of both brothers – pleading that his brother be spared.

The elder brother Robert remained at large hiding out in the wild woods that then covered the area until he was eventually captured in January and also taken to London for execution. It is probable that it was during this period that his wife gained her reputation for forlornly waiting for her husband to come home, endlessly walking the avenue of trees which became known as Lady Wintour's Walk. And so her shade continues on, endlessly waiting for the husband that never came home.

Chapter 2 – February

Jenkyn Place, Bentley, East Hampshire

Bentley is a small village in Hampshire, within which lies the small manor house Jenkyn Place. There are actually several villages bearing that name or similar around Hampshire, but the one which interests us lies not far to the west of Farnham. Today, the property is an award winning working vineyard which is not open to the general public but has occasional open days, and which specialises in two particular sparkling wines made with grapes grown on site.

The earliest reference to the site, in the Doomsday survey, lists "Janckenes Well", and it is believed this eventually corrupted to the name Jenkyn. The current house is a Grade II listed Queen Anne building.

The story is that a former housekeeper, known either as "Mrs Wagg" or as "Mrs Mopps". She is supposed to appear wearing a brown dress, white apron and "mob" cap, and carrying a lighted candle. She is most frequently seen during the month of February, and has been seen all over the house itself. Sometimes the moving candle is seen from outside the property – even at times when there is no-one actually at home.

She has apparently been seen within living memory by John Christie, who was the founder of the Glyndebourne Opera, and was also seen by some visitors in the early years of the Second World War, when the house was actually standing empty.

There is also supposed to be a tall white lady ghost haunting the path down to the bridge, and also a coach and horses haunting the courtyard leading in to the property.

Bournemouth, Dorset.

Just outside Bournemouth in Dorset, the A348 road passes over the River Stour by means of a bridge in the Longhams area. Between nearby Millhams Lane and this bridge, there is allegedly a ghostly lady in white, who was killed "many years ago" when hit by a horse and trap along the road. She is said to have sometimes tried to entice people to jump off the bridge, and was supposedly last seen in the 1970s. She only appears during February.

Unfortunately, no matter where I look, this is always the same version of the story that everyone quotes – I have found nowhere that gives any further information or any deviation from that version. Furthermore, the nearby road is not called Millhams *Lane* but is Millhams *Road*. This tends to suggest that everywhere this story is quoted comes from one original source – and this source is later than the 1970s. That seems odd to me if the lady was killed by a pony and trap since that would surely be from very early in the 1900s or even older? Which would beg the question – why does there only appear to be one mention of the story, endlessly repeated practically verbatim, from much later in time?

I'd be thrilled to hear from anyone who has actually seen this ghost, or has any more information.

February 8th

The Talbot Hotel, Oundle, Northamptonshire

Oundle is a picturesque small town in rural Northamptonshire. The Talbot Hotel is a Grade I listed building, parts of which date back to 638 a.d, and which has also at various times been named the Tabard or the Tabret. The first record of it as "The Talbot" dates back to 1617.

The main building still standing now was rebuilt in 1626, and some of the stonework which was used in its construction, as well as the main staircase, are said to come from nearby Fotheringhay Castle, where Mary Queen of Scots was held for a number of years before finally being executed on February 8th 1587.

Allegedly, the Queen walked down those very stairs on her way to her death, and it is this association which leads to claims that the royal ghost still haunts the building where those stairs are now located. Technically, the haunting is supposed to occur "predominantly in February" according to most sources, but I have set it against the actual date of her death as the most likely timeframe.

The stairs as they appear today certainly don't look sufficently ancient to date back far enough to actually be the original staircase from Fotheringhay, but as is often the case with restorations there may well be parts of it that are still the original oak. Furthermore, there seem to be no historical records detailing the sale of the staircase (or any other feature) to rebuild The Talbot.

Nevertheless, tradition holds that this did happen, and that Mary can be seen as a full apparition in one of the bedrooms, walking down the stairs wearing white, or heard weeping copiously. Legend also states that her executioner stayed at The Talbot the night before travelling on to nearby Fotheringhay to carry out his ghastly duty, and when doing so dined heartily on pigeon pie!

One paranormal investigation team visited the site in 2011, but recorded only some slight light anomalies which were slightly different from the normal dust/insect "orbs" which digital cameras routinely picked up. There was nothing within their investigation to either confirm or deny the presence of a ghost – let alone Mary Queen of Scots.

February 12th

Tower of London, London

The Tower of London needs no introduction, so firmly ensconced is it within history. One source claimed that a vague white shape can be seen flitting around the Tower of London on 12th February every year.

12th February is the day that Lady Jane Grey was beheaded in 1554. Only 17 years old, she spent just nine days as Queen of England before being deposed by Queen Mary – later to be known as Bloody Mary. Lady Jane Grey and her husband, Guildford Dudley, were imprisoned in the tower by the new Queen, and a few short months later Lady Jane had to watch her husband being led off to his execution before suffering the same fate herself.

February 13th

Goodwin Sands, English Channel, off Kent.

The legend is that on 13th February 1748, a schooner named "*Lady Lovibond*" foundered on the Goodwin Sands, just off the Kent coast between Deal and Dover. Most of the tales agree that the Captain had brought his newly wed wife on board for what was supposed to be a short voyage – and that it was the bad luck caused by having a woman on board which contributed to the tragedy.

Some tales say that the ship foundered due to negligence, some that it was bad weather, but most agree that the first seamen killed the pilot in a fit of jealousy over the Captain's marriage and then deliberately ran the ship aground. These types of stories hold a logical non sequitur for me: since everyone died on board (allegedly) then how can anyone have been left to tell the tale of what happened on board the ship that day?

Supposedly, the ghost of the schooner was first spotted fifty years to the day after its demise, in 1798, and its appearance was reported by two ships.

In 1848, so convinced were the witnesses that they were seeing a real schooner get into difficulties, that the lifeboats at Deal were called out to the wreck – only to find nothing there.
In 1898 there is no record of a sighting, but she was seen in 1948 "giving off an eerie green glow".
In 1998 quite a few would be ghost hunters and the media gathered to see if she would make an appearance – but to no avail.

The first written record for the *Lady Lovibond* dates from 1924 in the Daily Chronicle. There are no contemporary records of either the ship or its demise, and it is perhaps no coincidence that it is a story of love and jealousy attributable to the day before St Valentine's Day.

Interestingly, there are two other ghost ships in this area – the liner *SS Montrose*, and the Man'o'war *Shrewsbury*.

Glen Coe, Argyll, Scotland.

Glen Coe lies a few miles south of Fort William and Ben Nevis in the Scottish Highlands. A lonely, windswept place of immense natural beauty, it is also the site of one of the most tragic stories in British history.

In August 1691, King William III of England declared that all the highland chiefs must swear their loyalty to him by 31st January, or suffer the consequences.

The MacDonald clan of Glen Coe under their leader Alisdair were late signing the declaration by a couple of days, and the English King decided to make an example of their tardiness.

Troops were dispatched from Fort William, and they billeted themselves on the clan, who were forced to house and feed them and treat them with hospitality for around two weeks. In those days, billeting troops was heinously expensive and was probably designed to reduce the grain and food stores of the clan, and of course thus its disposable wealth.

Then on the night of February 13th, the troops attacked their hosts, killing 38 of the men while they were at rest. The remainder, including the women and children, fled into the unforgiving hills in terrible weather where around 40 more died of exposure or starvation after their settlement was put to the torch following the massacre.

The signed order which bade the attack is chilling even four hundred years later in its cold hearted wording:

You are hereby ordered to fall upon the rebels,
the McDonalds of Glenco, and put all to the sword under
seventy. You are to have a speciall care that the old Fox
and his sons doe upon no account escape your hands,
you are to secure all the avenues that no man escape.

This you are to putt in execution
att fyve of the clock precisely;
and by that time,
or very shortly after it, I'll strive to be att you
with a stronger party: if I doe not come to you
att fyve, you are not to tarry for me, but to fall on.

This is by the Kings speciall command,
for the good & safety of the Country, that these
miscreants be cutt off root and branch.

See that this be putt in execution without feud or favour,
else you may expect to be dealt with as one not true to
King nor Government, nor a man fitt to carry
Commissione in the Kings service.

*Expecting you will not faill in the full-
filling hereof, as you love your selfe,*

*I subscribe these with my hand
att Balicholis Feb: 12, 1692*

*(signed) R. Duncanson
For their Majesties service
To Capt. Robert Campbell of Glenlyon*

Today, it is said that if you visit the Glen in the early hours of that February morning, you will hear the screams and cries of the MacDonalds, or see vague shapes of people fleeing through the mists or hiding behind boulders.

One writer says that when driving through Glen Coe sometime in the early 1990's, he saw a young man with a wild and angry look about him wearing a traditional kilt and carrying a sword over his shoulder, striding along with bare feet a few metres from the road, with a woman in a dress and shawl struggling along behind him, also bare footed. He doesn't mention whether this happened to be in February, but he does describe the weather as cold and drizzling.

Many people still today write of the haunting and eerie feeling that pervades the Glen here.

February 15th

Hickling Broad / Potter Heigham, Norfolk

Potter Heigham is a small village on the River Thurne in Norfolk, famous for its medieval bridge and beloved as a busy tourist spot. It boasts tranquil boating holidays in its picturesque riverside setting or day boat hire for the casual visitor wishing to explore the waterways. There is also usually some very good sea-food and shellfish to be purchased.

In the bleak winter months, particularly February, it is also famous for its more sinister history – the haunting of the nearby Hickling Broad (a "broad" being where the river channels open out into an open area of water or lake) by the wraith of a drowned drummer boy.

The story goes that a young army drummer fell in love with a local lass from Potter Heigham whose father was reasonably well to do. He was aghast at the thought of his daughter courting with a mere soldier boy, and forbade the union.

The pair would therefore meet in secret, and often the young man would skate across the frozen river to keep the trysts with his lover. Sadly one February night the ice cracked as he skated across, and he fell to his death in the freezing waters. Supposedly, at around 7pm on February nights he can still be heard, forlornly playing his drum out across the misty waters, letting his lost love know that he is coming to meet her still.

Some versions of the tale place the tragedy at shortly prior to the time of the Battle of Waterloo which would make it February 1815 that he drowned. At least one author claims that the specific date of the event is February 15th. A lot of versions of the tale also put the drowning as taking place at a place called Swim Coots, by Hickling Broad. The story was being told at least as far back as 1890 by the writer Ernest Suffling, but he said the ghost had not been seen or heard for many years at that point in time.

February 24th

The Shrieking Pits, Northrepps, Norfolk.

Northrepps is a typical Norfolk village, set a just a little way inland from the coast and a few miles south of Cromer. Northrepp actually sits up on a plateau of sorts higher than the coast line, known as Hungry Hill, traversed by Hungry Hill Lane.

Somewhere off this lane lies an even smaller lane, and if you know which one to follow it will lead you to The Shrieking Pits – a gloomy hollow surrounded by trees and with a stagnant pool, which might possibly have originated as something to do with iron working in the area.

The story goes that there was once a young serving girl called Esmerelda, who at only 17 years old was exceptionally fair of face and fine of figure. Although she had many suitors, she set her cap at one of the local young farmers, even though he was already married and above her station in life. Hoping to one day somehow become his bride, she began a clandestine affair with him, and the pair would sneak around to meet one another secretly.

However, they obviously weren't cautious enough, for the local vicar caught wind of the affair and ordered them both to stop. To Esmerelda's despair, the farmer easily gave her up and returned to his wife – not wishing to cause himself a scandal or risk his wealth and good name. She is said to have either drowned herself in the pool now known as Shrieking Pit, or been lured there by something evil that sensed her distress. It is her desperate cries which can be heard marking the anniversary of her death.

Interestingly, there is another village called Aylmerton just a few miles away to the west of Cromer, which also boasts its own set of Shrieking Pits – and these also boast a tale of a ghostly woman in white seen bending over the pools and wailing as if in despair. That does rather beg the possibility that there are much older legends associated with these historical features which have transmuted over time into the current stories.

St Mary's Church, Bury St Edmunds, Suffolk.
The legend of the Grey Lady ghost seems to be quite a muddled one when looked at a little deeper.

She is said to haunt the grounds of St Marys Church, just next to the Abbey, every 24th February in penance for her wrongdoing. Some tales name her as Maude Carew, a nun at either the Abbey, St Mary's Church, a nearby priory, or the St Saviours Hospital, who murdered Humphrey, Duke of Gloucester, on that date in 1447.

However, historically there is no record of this: which seems a little strange considering that Humphrey was Humphrey of Lancaster, 1st Duke of Gloucester, 1st Earl of Pembroke, son of King Henry IV, brother of King Henry V, and uncle of King Henry VI.

What *is* known is that Humphrey took a second wife, Eleanor Cobham, who was arrested in 1441 and tried for sorcery – effectively ending Humphrey's public and political life. Humphrey himself was arrested on 20th February 1447 on a charge of treason, and died three days later on February 23rd. At the time, there were suspicions he had been poisoned, and when Shakespeare later wrote about him in his plays, he portrayed his death as having been ordered by Queen Margaret of Anjou.

It seems possible, according to some sources, that the actual story of Maude Carew as both the culprit and the subsequent ghost could be attributable to the imaginative mind of a Victorian printer's teenage daughter... a fact which supposedly came to light in 1861 when the good townspeople organised a ghost hunt on 24th February.

Nevertheless, there have been numerous sightings of a Grey Lady ghost all around this area for many years – and not confined to one date of the year.

St Saviours Hospital was built in 1180 and ceased to be a hospital in 1539. In those days hospitals were also used to house travellers.

Today all that remains if it is part of its front façade and an arched doorway. Behind that there is a modern day Tesco store, and this apparently has a lot of paranormal activity. As recently as 2006, astonished witnesses saw several cups of drink get knocked over by an unseen hand in the canteen area.

In the early 1970's a schoolgirl walking through the churchyard on her way home from St James School saw a hunched figure of an elderly lady in a long black dress and dark grey shawl by one of the graves who seemed to be there one second and inexplicably gone the next.

And so although it seems that the story of Maude and the date connection might have no truth – it does seem very likely that there is a Grey Lady ghost in the area – we will just never know who she really was and why she haunts.

February 26th

Hampton Court Palace, East Moseley, Surrey.

Hampton Court Palace needs little in the way of introduction, famous as it is, with being one of the Royal Palaces in England.

Sir Christopher Wren, the renowned architect who designed St Paul's Cathedral, lived in his later life in apartments within Hampton Court, which were allegedly given to him as part of the payment for his work on the great cathedral. In his 90th year he caught a chill and died on 26th February 1723.

Since then, it is said that on the anniversary of his death, his footsteps can be heard pacing up and down the stairs near to his chambers.

He is probably in good company as there seems to be quite a number of ghosts attached to Hampton Court, which is hardly surprising considering its long and rich history.

February 28th

Hathersage Vicarage, Hathersage, Derbyshire

One source that I have been able to find lists a seasonal ghost at the old Vicarage at Hathersage.

The vicarage was built in around 1673 originally and had various additions over the ensuing centuries. Once it had finished its time as a vicarage, it spent some years into the 1990s as a Bed and Breakfast business, but became a private property boasting six bedrooms which was last for sale in 2016 for just over £1 million.

It is allegedly haunted by a lady ghost who although not seen for the last hundred years or so, still allegedly opens one door in the house on this night in February.

I have not been able to find any record of why the date is significant, who the ghost is, or why the door is important. Although Charlotte Bronte stayed here in the early 1800s when visiting a friend, and perhaps drew inspiration for her tale Jane Eyre from a property she visited nearby, there is no particular link to her and the month of February.

Chapter Three - March

March 1st

Chapel of St Non, near St David's, Pembrokeshire, Wales

Overlooking the sea on the Pembrokeshire coast near the small town of St Davids sits the ruins of a medieval chapel thought to be dedicated to St Non, the mother of St David, patron saint for Wales.

Managed today by CADW (Welsh heritage), the picturesque ruins claim to be the birthplace of St David and certainly for much of its history the site was venerated as a Christian holy site.

It seems likely according to one source that there might have been a stone circle here even before the chapel, and that the site was important to the old Celtic faith before becoming a Christian place of pilgrimage.

According to some, the sound of chanting can still be heard either on St David's day (March 1st, the date of the Saints death in 589a.d) or on the evening before.
Near to the ruins is a natural spring well also dedicated to St Non and which is said to have healing properties.

Interestingly, after the site fell out of favour for pilgrimage following the protestant reformation, the site was a house for a while and then later used as a garden for growing leeks – also one of the national symbols of Wales.

March 11th

Loch Assynt, Sutherland, Scotland.

It is said that if you visit the shores of Loch Assynt on this date, you might hear the sound of a heavy blow, followed by running footsteps, followed by a splash.

Other versions say it is the sound of a thump, followed by running footsteps, panting, and a long drawn out sigh. One version says it occurs on March 19th.

All agree however, that you will be listening to the ghostly re-enactment of the sounds of a murder – when a local school teacher hit a pedlar over the head to kill him, stole his money, and threw the body in the Loch to disguise his crime.
The true story of the crime is almost as fascinating as it's haunting.

On 11th March 1830, there was a wedding at Little Assynt, which the locally well-known and liked pedlar Murdoch Grant attended, peddling his wares. He fared quite well from the gathering and left with his pockets jingling with coins.

He was never seen alive again.

About a month later, his badly decomposing corpse was found floating in nearby Loch Torr na h Eiginn. It was evident from the state of the body that there had been foul play, and the authorities from Inverness were sent for.

They focussed their interest in the local schoolmaster Hugh MacLeod, who it seems was a bit of a ne'er-do-well who had suddenly and suspiciously been spending a little extra cash.

Struggling to find hard evidence of his involvement, the authorities might have been stymied in their attempt to bring justice had not a local seer known as "Kenneth the Dreamer" stepped forward and claimed to have seen the vision of the murder in his dreams. Renewing their efforts, the authorities found evidence relating to the pedlar at Hugh MacLeod's home. He was duly tried, convicted, and hanged for the murder – apparently the only defendant in Scottish legal history whose conviction included the evidence from "second sight".

What is not explained by the accounts is – why is the haunting at Loch Assynt if the murder took place at Loch Torr na h Eiginn? The two are around five miles apart as the crow flies, (and probably nearer twenty by modern roads) and given the terrain it seems more than a little unlikely the body could have floated from one to the other down any linking water course?

March 14th

Hopton Castle, Hopton Heath, Shropshire

Hopton Castle, probably built in the late 1100s, attained notoriety in the English Civil War.

In February 1644 it was attacked by a large force of Royalists, but the garrison of around 30 Parliamentarian troops let by Samuel More, held out for around two or three weeks under siege until eventually the curtain wall was breached and all hope was lost. Samuel wrote a contemporaneous account of the events and his subsequent surrender and capture.
He records that he was offered safe passage for him and his remaining men (possibly around 28 souls) but to his lasting horror, whilst he himself was escorted safely away as a prisoner, his captors went against their word and put his men to death.

Some accounts say they were shot and then had their throats slit before being cast into a ditch.

Either way, on the anniversary of the massacre (sometimes recorded as 13th March), their ghosts are said to return to the castle, where they can be seen marching out of the ruin and gradually fading away from the ground upwards.

In the1990s, the remaining Keep of the castle was rapidly falling into ruin and oblivion, and local folk set up the Hopton Castle Preservation trust which bought it in 2008 and preserved it.

The popular television series Time Team investigated the castle in 2010, (series 17 episode 5 "The Massacre in The Cellars") but no human remains were found.

March 15th

Cley Hill, Wiltshire.

Cley Hill is a natural geographical feature not far from the town of Warminster in Wiltshire. Now held by the National Trust, it was once part of the Longleat Estate and is a place of spectacular natural beauty and wildlife. It also boasts an Iron Age hill fort and two Bowl Barrows.

Legend has it that the Devil dumped it there when he was intending to attack the town of Devizes by throwing the hill at them, but was he was duped into dropping his wearisome burden (and thus saving the town) by an old man he met walking along the road who told him that the town was so far away, that he himself had grown old whilst walking to reach it.

Today, Cley Hill has gained the reputation of being a UFO hotspot, where strange lights and sounds can be observed in the vast sky scape it affords. From as early as the 1960s there were reports – originally known as The Warminster Thing as it could often be heard as well as seen in the skies above the town.

In the 1970's, four local people driving past in a car saw regular bursts of light firing up from the hill into the clouds above. It's possible of course that these UFOs have more to do with the local military training area of Salisbury Plain.

For ghost hunters, its main interest lies in the wild looking figures chanting and dancing round a huge fire, which have been reported variously as recurring on March 15th, June 15th, October 31st and November 2nd. When investigations are later made, there is no sign of any real fire having been lit.
March 15th was important as a religious observances day in the Roman calendar, and was called the Ides of March. It later became one of the Christian Feast days – as did June 15th. October 31st is of course Halloween, and November 2nd is All Souls Day.

March 17th

The Old Ferryboat Inn, Holywell, Cambridgeshire

The Old Ferryboat Inn is a wonderfully situated pub, at the bottom of a dead end lane, with a pretty riverside garden, and which serves a particularly nice steak dinner. It might possibly be the oldest pub site in England, as it is said liquor has been sold from this site as far back as 560 a.d.

The legend goes that there used to be a beautiful 17 year of girl living in the village, called Juliet Tewsley. She fell in love with a local woodcutter (or forester) called Tom Zoul. Unfortunately, he scorned her love, and so, heartbroken, she either hanged herself or drowned herself in the Great Ouse River on March 17th 1050 a.d.

As suicide was a mortal sin, she was buried in unhallowed ground close to the river, and her grave was marked by a simple stone slab.

Over the years, as buildings changed and expanded, eventually the stone slab became part of the flooring of the pub itself.

It is said that every anniversary of her death her spirit rises at midnight. Some versions say she rises from the slab and goes to the river - other versions have it the other way around. In 1982 one writer claimed that she never failed to appear, but despite this assertion there don't appear to be any actual eyewitness accounts.

There is a Youtube video of an investigation from 2007 by a paranormal group.

My husband and I visited the pub for a late dinner on March 17th 2017. It wasn't particularly busy, but there were flyers laid out on each table giving the history of the ghost legend. We had our two Belgian Malinois dogs with us in the hope they might react to anything paranormal, but they were much more interested in putting on their best puppy dog eyes and charming our fellow diners out of bits of sausage and steak.

Our waitress told us she had never seen or felt anything unusual there, but whenever something odd happened like a piece of equipment failing or something going missing, the staff will tend to say "oh it must be the ghost" even now.

The only slightly odd thing we saw was that as the hour grew late and people left, we were left sitting alone in a nook area that housed four or five tables. Each table had a candle lit, which was a small candle wedged into the neck of a decorative glass bottle and tied with a little bow of hessian type ribbon. As we sat there, suddenly each candle on the tables all guttered and died within a three or four second period of each other.

It was probably more to do with uniformity of candle size than the paranormal, but it was a little bit odd to watch them all gutter and drop through the necks of their respective bottles at practically the same time.

March 22nd

Tower of St John's, Ayr, Scotland

The Tower of St John's in Ayr was originally built around 900 years ago – so it is probably hardy surprising that it picked up a ghost or two.

Robert the Bruce held parliament here in 1315, and although originally a church and church tower, it was rebuilt into a defensive tower in the same century. Today, it is situated on a small but well-kept patch of green between Eglington Terrace and Bruce Crescent, and looks strangely out of place amongst the neat little rows of houses which surround it. Normally closed to the public, it does usually have an opening day in September.

The haunting which occurs on 22nd March is said to be that of a grey figure of a man – and he seems to be listed variously as a monk, a builder, or a warrior figure: but nowhere can I find any trace of why he is supposed to haunt. Neither can I find any stories of anyone actually seeing the ghost – and so far I have only found one primary source.

March 24th

Ballyseede Castle, Tralee, Ireland

Now a beautiful country hotel set in 300 acres, Ballyseede Castle in Ireland is allegedly haunted by one if its former residents on 24th March each year.

The original building dated from the 16th century, and was the chief garrison of the Earls of Desmond. The Last Earl of Desmond, Gerald Fitzgerald, refused to swear his allegiance to the crown and was eventually captured and beheaded in 1583.

Ballyseede was then forfeited in 1590 to the Blennerhassett family, who remodelled in 1627.

There was a terrible massacre close to the boundary of the castle 9 March 1923, where 9 IRA prisoners were bound and made to stand in front of a barricade – which was then detonated with explosives, killing all nine.

The last of the Blennerhassett incumbents at Ballyhede, the spinster Hilda, who died in December 1965 apparently now haunts her beloved home. She was on active service as a nurse in the First World War and was one of the very few women to be awarded the 1914 Mons Star medal.

After Hilda died, she bequeathed Ballyseede to a cousin, Sir Adrian Blennerhassett, who sold the property in 1967. There seems to be no particular significance to link Hilda to this particular date in March. Furthermore, many reports suggest that actually, her ghost is active all year round.

One story alleges that a group of residents left the hotel (variously reported as 1988 or 1998) having seen Hilda and refused to return to their rooms. Another says a worker there refused ever to enter a certain bedroom again having witnessed a wardrobe door opening and closing itself with force.

In 2014/15, the TV series Ghost Circle aired an episode about an investigation at the castle.

March 29th

Cheriton Woods, Cheriton, near Alresford, Hampshire

Near the small village of Cheriton, just south of Alresford in Hampshire, lies Cheriton Woods, which although privately owned now were actually the site of one of the most bloody battles of the English Civil War on 29 March 1644. Although a decisive victory for the parliamentarians, over 300 men died that day in hard fought bloody combat.

Legend has it that on the anniversary of the battle every four years, you can either hear the sounds of the battle or even see the soldiers marching by. However, I have found various versions giving the "cycle" as last due in 2014, 2015, or 2016 - so actually it seems equally likely that you stand a good chance on any given year of having some sort of experience there. Given that the woods are privately owned, you will need to respect the rules under the Countryside and Rights Of Way Act if you decide to do a spot of ghost hunting of your own.

The earliest record seems to come from nearby Hinton Ampner House (now long gone with only the gardens remaining) from 1771. At this time, it is said the lady of the house grew so perturbed by the endless nights of fear and unrest at the house with the apparitions of an old man and an old woman, and the sounds of a battle raging nearby, that she packed up her children and belongings and fled.

Eventually the house was abandoned and fell into ruin because no one could stand to stay there with the gruesome noises continuing in the night. This record also gives weight to the theory that the activity is not relegated to one night only.

Much more recently, around 1970, one writer recounts his own experience there. He was at that time part of a civil war re-enactment society, and they decided to stage a re-enactment in and around the village on the anniversary of the battle. For the latter end of their busy day, they staged a last march through a sunken greenway between two high hedgerows locally known as "The Lane of Disaster" since it was here that a particularly vicious skirmish took place with huge casualties.

As he and his fellow re-enactment "soldiers" marched out of the lane in the gathering dusk and headed towards the pub, one of the villagers watching and cheering them on asked where the "other" side of the army were going to go for a drink. When questioned about what he meant by that – it quickly transpired that he had seen another small army of silent soldiers march out just ahead of the re-enactors... and had naturally just assumed they were part of the day's entertainments.

In March 2011 one set of ghost hunters visited the site on the anniversary, and had several strange experiences including a dark shape caught on camera and hearing the sounds of musket shots and men crying out coming from within the woods.

As a gruesome side note, a legend at nearby Kilmeston Manor says that when a carpenter removed some wood panelling in order to install a new inset cabinet, to his horror he found the perfectly preserved body of a cavalier soldier walled in behind the panelling. Apparently, as the air hit the corpse, the flesh crumbled to dust, leaving only the skeleton behind...

Chapter 4 - April

April 2nd

Ludham bridge, Norfolk

The source story for this haunting says that when visiting Norfolk around 90 years ago and stopping at Ludham bridge for supplies, Dr Charles Sampson happened to speak to an old historian there.

He was told the legend of the Viking raid which is re-enacted every 2nd April, after full night has settled over the quiet river. He supposedly returned the following year and moored his boat with a few trusted companions on board near to the fateful spot, and settled down to spend the night watching the spot.

Their wait was rewarded when some cattle in the neighbouring field suddenly became very spooked, and suddenly started stampeding towards the river. It quickly became apparent that they were fleeing from the party of mounted riders blowing hunting horns and cracking whips as they drove the cattle ahead of them towards the river.

The whole spectacle came close to overrunning the moored boat, but at the last crucial second before the cattle could have flung themselves into the river, the whole scene disappeared – including the cattle!

As you get further into this book, you will perhaps become as sceptical as I about any tales from the book by Charles Sampson. I haven't been able to find any other sightings or reports of paranormal activity for this bridge.

April 4th

Rochester Castle, Kent

Rochester Castle stands on the eastern bank of the River Medway in Kent and was originally built by Gundulf, Bishop of Rochester, in 1087, but like all castles it was added to and modified over the centuries.

The story of the ghost dates back to 1264, when April 4th fell at Easter (some versions say Good Friday). Unsurprisingly, considering it is such an ancient tale, there seems to be several slight variations to how it is told.

All agree, however, that the ghost of a lady in white is that of Blanche De Warren (some versions say de Warenne).

Most versions claim that during the siege of the castle that year, she was struck by an arrow and killed. Variations on how that came about say that she was either inadvertently struck when an arrow ricocheted off a defending knight's armour whilst she was visiting the battlements, or more romantically, she was inadvertently pierced through the heart when a rogue knight called Gilbert de Clare from the opposing army snuck into the castle and tried to kidnap her. He was seen by her fiancé Ralph de Capo from the courtyard below who fired the arrow to kill De Clare and thus to save her, but it bounced off De Clare's breastplate and pierced poor Blanche instead.

Some versions say she fell from her window after being struck, some say de Clare chased her up onto the battlements before the tragedy happened and she fell from there. Some versions say she actually flung herself to her death to avoid his attentions.

Interestingly, history records that Gilbert de Clare, 7th Earl of Rochester was busy attacking the Jewish population at Canterbury in April 1264 – so it does sound as if he had a busy month that year...

An investigation held at the castle in 1992 by ASSAP heard unexplained footsteps coming down the main stairs at 4.25am, whilst in December 2007 a visitor claimed to have seen a lady in medieval clothing walking down the same staircase.
In 2010, another visitor heard a disembodied woman's voice whisper close to their ear, so it's always possible that Lady Blanche is still active.

April 7th

Acle Bridge, Acle, Norfolk

The legend of the haunting of Acle bridge is quite colourful, to say the least.

The story goes that in the first quarter of the 17th Century, one Josiah (or John or Joshua, depending which version you read) Burge was a local corn chandler (a type of merchant) in Acle. He was said to be a cruel and unpleasant man who starved his children and beat his wife.

One fateful day, he took the beatings too far and his long suffering wife died from the wounds he inflicted on her. Knowing that he would be put on trial, he bribed the local doctor to swear in court that she had died of natural causes, and so he was acquitted of her murder.

However, her brother (whose name does not seem to appear anywhere) knew what a cruel man his sister had been saddled with, and felt certain that she had met her demise at the hands of her husband. Determined to exact revenge for her loss, he waited for Josiah to return home one night.

As Joshua crossed Acle Bridge, the brother leapt out and cut his throat from ear to ear – so that Joshua fell to the ground in the middle of the bridge and bled to death.

The brother knew that he would be the main suspect for the murder and so fled the country, boarding a ship at nearby Great Yarmouth. Unfortunately, the authorities arrested and tried one Jack Ketch who had reason to hold a grudge against Josiah for some business dealings gone awry, and hanged the poor innocent man for a crime he had nothing whatsoever to do with.

The brother eventually returned some years later and learned of the death of the innocent man. Overcome with guilt, he returned to the scene of the crime one night, where the ghost of Josiah rose towards him through the murky water below. The next morning the brother's body was found dangling from the bridge, with his throat partially cut through.

Many of the villagers believed the spirit of Josiah Burge had taken its own revenge – others believed that possibly it was the spirit of the wrongfully accused Jack Ketch. Personally I question how anyone knows that the ghost rose through the water when no-one left that bridge alive that night if it was just the ghost and the brother. And why would the ghost be in the water anyway? Why not just waiting on the bridge itself?

If there is any truth that the brother did in fact die on the bridge as described, then it was perhaps an act of remorseful suicide, or even yet another act of revenge from someone else in Josiah's family.

As a result of the tragedy, every 7th April, a pool of blood is said to appear on Acle Bridge. It allegedly still happens despite the bridge being rebuilt in the 1830's, 1931, and again in 1997.

Interestingly, there *was* a John Ketch who died in 1686, who was known as Jack Ketch.

He was an executioner who was known for his callowness towards his victims, and whose botched and cruel executions became notorious during his lifetime and ever after.

So notorious was he in fact, that the name "Jack Ketch" came to be synonymous with "death", "Satan" or "execution"... and one can't help but speculate that this is how the name has become woven into this tale when the name of the poor wife and the revengeful brother seem to have been lost.

On Thursday April 7th 2016 "Out There Paranormal TV" conducted an investigation which can be viewed on Youtube on the bridge and probably unsurprisingly found no trace of blood.

April 9th

Orme House, Newport, Isle of Wight

This is quite an elusive tale, but I shall give you what little I have found.

Orme House is on Pyle Street in Newport on the Isle of Wight. It seems to be a children's nursery currently, but that is all I have been able to find out about the building.

Two sources say that the location is haunted every 9th April by the ghost of an old lady – one version mentions she is wrapped in a shawl.

One version says she was seen in 1985 and again in 1992 - but neither source gives any further information as to who she was in life or why she haunts. If anyone can elucidate further – email me!

April 12th

St Mary's Church, Hinckley, Leicestershire

There has been a church on this site for around 900 years – so it is hardly surprising it has picked up a legend or two.

The most famous is certainly that of the bleeding tombstone.

The legend goes that on 20th April 1727 a recruiting sergeant had visited the town and was talking to a crowd in the market place, trying to convince people of the virtue of "taking the King's shilling", as joining the armed forces was once known.

Unfortunately his impassioned speech kept being interrupted by a young likely lad aged 20, called Robert Smith, who worked as a saddler in the town. Robert was having fun making quips and poking fun at the sergeant much to the amusement of the gathered crowd – but to the growing annoyance of the sergeant.

Eventually the sergeant lost his temper, and gave the crowd a demonstration of how effective the weapons of war could be – by running poor Robert through with his halberd (a form of pike with a blade on one end).

Richard was buried in St Mary's church, and the inscription on his gravestone reads:

> *A fatal Halbert his mortal body slew*
> *The murdering hand God's vengeance will pursue*
> *From shades terrestrial though justice took her flight*
> *Shall not the judge of all earth do right*
> *Each age and sex his innocence bemoans*
> *And with a sad sigh laments his dying groans*

Ever since then, on the night of his murder, the tombstone is said to still bleed with grief at the sorrow of his young life taken away for such a minor transgression.

In 1936 one researcher suggested that one of the reasons the gravestone might be seen to exude a reddish substance was its positioning at that time below a red sandstone block in the east chancel window.

Whatever the truth, the story goes back at least as far as 1874 when it was cited in the Leicester Chronicle according to one source.

April 14th

Roughtor, Cornwall

On 14th April 1844, a young servant girl from Penhale Farm called Charlotte Dymond was murdered, and a few days later her body was discovered near Roughtor on Bodmin Moor – her throat had been slit.

She had been courting a fellow servant called Matthew Weekes, who supposedly killed her in a fit of jealousy when she started to show interest in the farmer's son, Thomas Prout.

Matthew fled the area for Plymouth, but was caught and tried for the murder, eventually meeting his death by hanging at Bodmin Gaol on 12th August 1844.

Since then, it is said that her spirit can be seen around the site of her murder at the anniversary, wearing a bright red shawl and a bonnet. Sometimes she is just seen as a distant figure in white.

In 2011, a local paranormal group investigated the site on the anniversary, and details of the investigation and the two loud screams they managed to capture on tape can be found in Jason Higgs' book *Haunted Bodmin Moor*.

Jason does comment that it was possibly the call of a fox (which can sound remarkably like human screams sometimes) – but it was also possibly the sound of Charlotte's last screams.

Another paranormal investigator tried in 2014 but had no luck.

April 16th

Drummossie Moor, Culloden, Scotland

April 16th 1746 saw the brief but exceptionally bloody battle near Culloden on Drummossie Moor where the Jacobite forces of Bonny Prince Charlie were defeated for the last time, and thousands of clansmen lost their lives either in the heat of battle or were slaughtered as they lay wounded afterwards.

Ever since, the site is said to be haunted by the sounds of the battle – men crying, clashing steel and the beat of military drums. Occasionally the spectre of a lone highlander picking his weary way across the moor is glimpsed, and some say that if you can get close enough before he disappears, he can be heard to say "defeated!" in a forlorn and weary whisper. Another legend says that the site is haunted by a huge black bird known as The Scree of Culloden, and to see it is bad luck as it is considered a harbinger of doom.

Yet another legend says that heather will not grow on the site – but unfortunately that particular claim can be laid to rest simply by looking at any modern day photos taken there.

In 2007 Scottish Paranormal investigated the site and recorded strange anomalous fluctuations in both temperature and humidity around the sites of the graves – but not anywhere else in the vicinity where the readings held consistent with the weather conditions on the day.

In 2014 an American paranormal group investigated the site and recorded two "EVP"s. The two EVPs were recorded as a voice saying, "who died here?" and "here they come!"

EVP stands for "Electronic Voice Phenomena". This is where a tape recorder or other recording device picks up human voices even though nothing was heard at the time by the actual investigator holding the recording device.

It is a different phenomenon to that of the sound of a disembodied voice actually heard by someone present at the time, which also shows up on a recording device.

So if you happen to be visiting there on your holidays pop the voice recorder on your phone on as you walk around – you never know who might be walking round with you.

April 24th

Smithills Hall, Bolton, Lancashire

There has been a manor here at Smithills Hall since at least 1335, but our ghost dates back to 24th April 1555. The building today is a museum with free entry.

In 1554 a local farmer named George Marsh, who had become a preacher after the death of his wife, was arrested and brought to Smithills Hall for questioning, before being sent on for trial. He was accused of heresy – specifically of preaching and practising the Protestant faith under the reign of Catholic Queen Mary I of the Tudor dynasty.

Legend says that he was so incensed at his treatment that he stamped his foot so hard he left an imprint of his boot in the flagstone floor in the entrance to the Withdrawing room.

He was then sent away to Lancaster Gaol for trial, was convicted, and subsequently burned at the stake in Boughton near Chester on 24th April 1555 after refusing to recant his faith during his period of imprisonment.

Ever since, on the anniversary of his death, the mark he left in the floor becomes bloodied in recognition of his martyrdom for his faith. Today, the mark is protected by a glass covering.

The building itself is said to be fairly well active with paranormal happenings all year round. Visitors have reported the figure of a man seen in the Green Room, where George was questioned. Others have seen the ghostly form of a man apparently kneeling in prayer in the chapel. People working on the site have reported that glasses or other small objects are sometimes overturned or moved around when the museum is closed up for the night.

Unexplained footsteps have been heard coming from the stairs when no-one is there, and the sound of children giggling sometimes drifts through when no living children are present. In 2007 a local news reporter spent the night in there as part of an organised ghost investigation, but remained unconvinced that anything paranormal had occurred.

Barmby Moor, Yorkshire

Barmby Moor is a small village to the east of York, not to be confused with the similarly named but further south, not far from Sheffield, Barnby Moor.

According to legend, there was a Quaker Burial ground in the garden of one of the houses, and if you went there on St Marks Eve – 24th April – and turned around 7 times, then the figure of a man would appear behind you.

There was certainly a licensed Quaker meeting house in the village in 1707, but other than that there appears to be very little more detail about this legend anywhere I could find.
It is very likely therefore to be a localised corruption of the superstition which was very prevalent in England, but particularly in Yorkshire, in the 1700s onwards.

Most versions of the superstition hold that if one were to visit a church on St Mark's Eve, and sit quietly in the porch between the hours of 11.00pm to 1.00am, one would see the apparitions of those who were going to die in the coming year walk into the church.

Some versions say that one must hold this vigil for the three nights leading up to St Mark's Eve, and others that one must circle around the church before taking up the watching position.

Church of St Mary and St Andrew, Whittlesford, Cambridgeshire

This is another church which holds the same legend as that at Barmby Moor. Apparently, though, in Cambridgeshire the ghosts are a little more specific as they like to march into the churchyard and lay down in the spot where they will be buried, before fading from sight.

Certainly the superstition is a long lasting one, as in 1905 one G.N.Maynard wrote that almost a hundred years earlier, some locals decided to keep the vigil to see if it was true. Unfortunately, some of their friends thought it would be funny to play the part of the ghosts, and at the appointed hour came creeping into the churchyard and frightened the watchers so badly they ran away – tripping and falling onto graves themselves as they ran.

St Mary's Churchyard, Scarborough, North Yorkshire

And finally for this date, another church with the same tradition. To add a twist though, local legend says that in 1786 one lady was taking the role of one of the hopeful watchers trying to witness the phenomenon when to her horror she saw a phantasm of herself walk into the church! She became so terrified that she collapsed and died from the fright – thus bringing about her own self-fulfilling prophecy.

There is a video taken by some ghost hunters on Youtube who held the vigil on 24th April 2010 and felt they were getting some strange static feelings and some shadow figures glimpsed. It's possibly slightly spoiled by one of them chatting with his Mum on the phone at the same time....or perhaps that just demonstrates they uploaded their whole video as it was, without editing it.

St Mary's church is also said to be haunted more generally – by a figure who can be seen moving about the graveyard as an indistinct shadow.

April 26th

Penfound Manor, Poundstock, Cornwall

Located a little way south of Bude, this ancient manor house boasts itself as the oldest continually inhabited family home in Britain. Built around a medieval hall with later additions, it is still privately owned by the Penfound family.

As such, it is not really possible to say whether the ghosts are still haunting since it is not open to the public.
Nevertheless, the story is that during the English Civil War, Kate Penfound, whose family were Royalists, fell in love with John Trebarfoot, whose family were Parliamentarians. Knowing that given the political divide between their families they would never be allowed to marry, they decided to elope on 24th April 1643, or 1648, or 1650 (depending on which version you happen to be reading!)

Unfortunately, Kate's father caught the two in the act of trying to leave the manor, and a sword fight ensued between the two men in the courtyard. John was fatally stabbed in the fight, and as Kate ran to try and save him, she was also caught in the sword play and wounded. Both she and her father died a few days later of their injuries.

Allegedly, Kate's ghost can be seen flitting around the manor at any time of year, but on the 24th April the ghostly duel is re-enacted in the courtyard.

April 27th

Burgh Castle, Near Great Yarmouth, Norfolk

Burgh castle was built by the Romans as part of their network of coastal defences, and housed the Stablesian Cavalry unit, who originated from Greece, for a time. It was an imposing stone walled garrison, where the 4.5 meter high walls enclosed an area of approximately 6 acres. Today only three of the walls are still standing as the fourth has crumbled into the encroaching marshes over the centuries. Managed now by English Heritage it is open to the public with free entry during daylight hours and boasts lovely views across the marshes and the mere.

The legend is that a Danish warlord was holding the fort when the Saxons came to recapture it. Their leader was taken prisoner, and died on 27th April 418 a.d. The messenger who came to broker his release was flung from the battlements with a white cloth which had been used to strangle him tied around his neck.

Ever since then, the sounds of the men screaming in battle and the clash of swords can be heard on the anniversary. Sometimes, something white can be seen falling from the battlements.

At other times of the year there is also a Black Shuck, known locally as Old Scarfe, which is said to roam the ruins. Black Shucks are spectral black dogs or "hell hounds" which are common in English folklore in Southern Britain and which are said to bring bad luck to those who see them. Tales of them may well relate back to the War Hounds of Odin tales that the Viking raiders brought with them.

Sometimes visible too are the ghost of a young urchin in rags, a Roman solider, and a man walking a dog.

Numerous paranormal societies have investigated the site including RA Paranormal & Supernatural, and Eastern Counties Paranormal Investigators.

Paul Nichols uploaded a photo to the popular social media site Flickr on 27.09.2013 which showed the sun setting over Burgh Castle, and in which he feels there is a stern looking face showing in the clouds. I can't actually make out any face at all – but it is nevertheless a nice photo.

April 30th

Burrough Green, Cambridgeshire

Although not actually a haunting, I have included this entry just out of interest.

Just south of Newmarket lies the small village of Burrough Green. The primary school there was funded as far back as 1630 when Dr Anthony Gage decreed that the rent from a designated parcel of land should be used to provide a school room and a teacher to teach the children basic reading and writing.

The building has been a school ever since, but of course it has been expanded on over the years. The first main expansion came in 1730, and parts of this building still stand – including the two carvings of a boy and a girl in period dress above the original front door.

Legend says that on the evening of April 30th, the statues hop down from their perches and dance around the village green – sometimes even leaving behind their footprints as proof.

I have been unable to find any particular origin for the legend – the oldest mention I can find dates from 1978. However, April 30th is May Day Eve – and even today the school maintains a tradition of dancing around the maypole May Day, so the legend might just relate to this. Alternatively, since April 30th is Walpurgis Night, a date associated with witches, perhaps the origins of the legend are tied up with that.

Chapter 5 – May

May 1st

Definitely a bumper day for anniversary hauntings, May 1st is traditionally the May Day festival, or going back further in time, the Beltane festival – both religious festivals associated with the time of the year as the halfway point between the spring equinox and midsummer.

Loch Ashie, near Inverness, Scotland

Not far from Inverness and the more famous Loch Ness, Loch Ashie boasts a recurring ghostly battle.

Although there are no historical records of any battle taking place here, legend says that it was the site of a mighty battle between the Gaels (led by Fingal) and the Norse (led by A'ishidh, after whom the Loch is named), and certainly there are many sites around the Loch named for the battle.

Sightings of it seem to have been around for well over a hundred years – when it was reported in the 1870/71 period it was even suggested it could have been a mirage thrown from the faraway fighting in the Franco Prussian war.

Sometimes it is reported as a full scale battle with lines of soldiers and cavalry, other times just a handful of ancient looking Clansmen in battle kilts running through the mists with short swords and wooden clubs.

It was seen during the First World War, twice between the end of the Second World War and the 1960s, and was reported again in 2012 by six tourists camping near the Loch.

In 2001 two ghost hunters visited the site but found themselves trespassing on a Scottish Water installation, and drawing the attention of the night-watchman there. The police were duly called and were slightly amused at the antics of the intrepid hunters. It does at least demonstrate the importance of having proper permission to be on site if you want to do a spot of ghost hunting anywhere.

Godstow Chapel, Wolvercote, Oxfordshire

Godstow chapel is all that remains of the original nunnery which was funded in the twelfth century by Elvida, the widow of Sir William Launceline of Winchester. It was once quite an impressive conglomeration of buildings before falling into disuse, but today only the ruined outer walls of the private chapel remain standing.

Allegedly, just before dawn on the first of May each year, it is possible to hear the sounds of the nuns still singing and chanting.

It also said to be haunted by Rosamund Clifford, the long term mistress of King Henry II. She died in 1176, and some believed that her death was brought about at the command of the jealous Queen Eleanor.

South Walsham Broad, Norfolk.

South Walsham is a picturesque Norfolk broadlands village situated just to the north west of Acle. Next to it lies one of the open areas of the river route ways known as a Broad – hence this particular stretch is called South Walsham Broad.

The legend goes that on the 1st May every year, a burning Viking longboat can be seen drifting across the broad itself and slowly sinking out of sight.

I have been unable to find any record of anyone actually seeing it – which is quite strange considering what a popular holiday destination the broads are, and how many rented holiday boats must have been moored in the area of South Walsham broad on any given May 1st.... one would think at least one holidaymaker would have noticed if a ship on fire drifted slowly past...

Certainly Viking raids were a real problem in this area right up until the latter end of the 9th century, when the raiders defeated the resident Anglo-Saxon king and took control of the land - where many Vikings then settled and no doubt brought their traditions with them. One such custom was the cremation of their dead on funeral pyres, where it was believed the smoke would carry their spirit safely to the afterlife. For certain high born folk, or great warriors, sometimes this cremation was formed by setting them adrift in a blazing boat: usually though this would be done at sea, rather than a relatively speaking smallish inland body of water – and with the sea so close by in this instance it does seems a little odd that they would choose here instead of the open sea.

On the other hand, if this is a re-enactment, or even just a long-surviving folk memory, it could be that a Viking raiders' boat was set on fire as part of the fighting. The folk memory is perhaps reflected in the village name sign, which shows a Viking longboat.

Burgh Castle, Norfolk

We have already visited Burgh Castle in April for an anniversary haunting – and here it is again with its apparently busy calendar!

According to one source, on the 1st May each year it is possible to see the castle reflected in the water of the mere not as it is today – but resplendent in all its former glory with pennants flying and walls intact.

Lynn Cwm Llwch, Brecon Beacons Mountains, South Wales

This next tale is not actually a haunting, but I've included it out of interest.

Lynn Cwm Llwch is a remote lake formed by retreating glaciers high up in the range of mountains known as the Brecon Beacons. The lake is an area Of Special Scientific Interest and sits below the two highest peaks – a beautiful, wild, rugged area which is difficult to reach except on foot.

Legend says that there is actually an invisible island in the centre of the lake inhabited by the Faerie realm where they live in a beautiful garden hidden from mortal eyes. However, once a year, a portal will open in a rock on the lake shore, and should you choose to pass through the craggy doorway, you will find yourself on the island visiting the fair folk.

Most versions, however, go on to say that many years ago one foolhardy mortal tried to steal an exotic flower from the island, which angered the faeries who struck him senseless, and he remained a gibbering wreck for the rest of his life. The faeries now mostly refuse to open the portal – probably quite sensible if your house guests are going to be rude enough to try and steal from you.

River Wharfe, Yorkshire

Along one stretch of the River Wharfe, not far from Bolton, lies one of the most dangerous water courses in the country – known as The Strid.

Here the river, which is about 40 feet wide, is forced to pass through a natural rock channel which is only about 4 feet wide at its narrowest point. Unsurprisingly, this causes the water to run at a phenomenal speed through the restricted channel, and the action has caused the river to cut ever deeper through the rock below – no-one knows exactly how deep it goes, but it is thought it may have carved out subterranean chambers.

Unfortunately, because the river looks so narrow here, the foolhardy have been known to try and jump across it at this rocky juncture. All is well if they land surefootedly on the other side – but it is claimed that no-one who has fallen in has ever survived the fall. Some reports say that some bodies are never even found – hence the suspicion of underwater chambers.

There are two principle legends relating to the 1st May and this area of water. One is that a white horse will rise out of The Strid bearing the Queen of Faeries on his back, and they will try to entice the unwary back into the waters with them.

Another is that a courting couple betrothed to be wed once met here – he on one side of the bank, she on the other. When she tried to leap across to join her beau she missed her footing and was swept away to her death – followed by her lover who leapt in to try and save her. To this day, her mournful cries can be heard over the sound of the rushing water every May Day.

In a horrible twist of fate, a couple on their honeymoon in August 1998 died in a flash flood at the Strid when the water seems to have rapidly risen and swept them to their deaths. The body of the man was not found until the October, and was ten miles downstream.

May 2nd

St Mary the Virgin Church, Burgh St Peter, Norfolk

Burgh St Peter is a pleasant village not far from Lowestoft in Norfolk. Its church boasts an unusual tiered tower – in the shape which some say is reminiscent of a wedding cake or of an eastern ziggurat.

The church was built in the 13th century, and some original parts still remain, but its tower was built in the late 1700s. There are various versions to the legend of the ghost in the graveyard – but all seem to agree on the date of 2nd May.

The legends seem also to mostly agree that the story started with one Adam Morland, described variously as the founder of the church, a wealthy landowner, or a poor farmer. Either way, it is claimed that he borrowed money from the Devil – either to build the church or just to enhance his own wealth - and in return he agreed that the Devil would take his soul upon his death.

Adam died on 2nd May, but had his body buried in the consecrated ground of the church so that the Devil couldn't take his soul. Every anniversary, the Devil visits the churchyard disguised as an old man, trying to get to Adam.

Another version says the ghost is in fact Adam – who is unable to leave the church without forfeiting himself to the clutches of the Devil.

Curiously, when you think about it – almost every person was buried within the consecrated grounds of a church, so why should this save Adam particularly? Surely if one were to believe in such – then his soul was in danger the moment he died – not after he was buried. Perhaps the missing part of the legend is that he made sure he *died* within the bounds of the church... and has been unable to leave ever since.

May 4th

Shaw Green Lane, Prestbury, Gloucestershire

Prestbury lies just north of Cheltenham in Gloucestershire, and often claims the title of most haunted village in England. It is perhaps fitting then that one of its many ghosts should claim a particular date of the year.

This is the ghost of a medieval rider – usually seen only in misty outline form, or even just heard as the sound of galloping hooves.

The legend is that he was a messenger trying to reach the camp of King Edward IV at Tewkesbury during the War of the Roses, who was shot down by an arrow as he galloped through the village.

Certainly, 4th May is the date of the Battle of Tewkesbury in 1471, so it is entirely likely that messengers would have been frantically riding to give orders or news.

Some versions of the tale state that in 1901 roadworks were taking place at the northern end of the village and the men working there discovered a skeleton with an arrowhead still lodged between its ribs... possibly the mortal remains of the hapless messenger?

I haven't been able to find any actual accounts of recent sightings of it – but several accounts claim that it is the only ghost in Prestbury which is still known to be active.

May 12th

Salthouse, Norfolk

Salthouse is a small village on the north Norfolk coast, not far from Sheringham, situated on the salt marshes.

There is a legend that on 12th May each year, at "Salthouse Pool" in the late evening it is possible to witness the spectral re-enactment of a medieval (or possibly Roman) feast – with bonfires, singing and dancing. Some versions say it is the third Tuesday of May.

I haven't been able to find any other sources to give any more detailed information about this haunting, nor of when it might last have been witnessed.

Interestingly, there doesn't seem to be a specifically named "Salthouse Pool" at Salthouse – although there are certainly tidal pools in the marshes. There is however a water course called Salthouse Pool near Barrow in Furness in Cumbria.

Historically, Richard the Lionheart, King Richard I, was married in France on May 12th 1191a.d. and did have lavish feasts celebrating his nuptials, so it is possibly one of these happy festivities that echoes down the centuries?

May 19th

Blickling Hall and the Bridges to Wroxham, Norfolk

I have grouped all these alleged hauntings together, as they all relate to the same historical incident.

To understand the sheer impact of the historical facts behind the alleged hauntings, a short history lesson is needed. King Henry VIII of England is forever famous for the well-known fact that he had six wives, and the rhyme *"Divorced, Beheaded, Died, Divorced, Beheaded, Survived"* has been learned by rote by countless school children. Many people will automatically remember that Anne Boleyn was the second wife, and was beheaded.

Perhaps a little less known is just how utterly scandalous and far reaching the antics of King Henry towards his unfortunate wives actually was: especially in the light of the very religious society prevalent at the time.

Henry had been married to his first wife for 24 years before he set her aside in favour of Anne. Divorce was not allowed under the religious rules of the time, so he changed the entire religion of his country in order to get his way. He and the young Anne (she was probably in her mid-twenties) first married in secret in January 1533, but by June that same year he had made sufficient legal and religious changes as to be able to officially crown her as Queen of England at a lavish ceremony in Westminster Abbey.

The timeline leading up to the fateful day of Anne's beheading on 19th May 1536 (just three short years later) makes truly chilling reading.

On 2nd May, the first arrests were made.

On 12th May, Mark Smeaton (a musician at court), William Brereton and Francis Weston (both courtiers) and Sir Henry Norris (personal body servant and friend to the King) were charged and found guilty of adultery with the Queen.

On 15th May, Anne and her brother George, Lord Rochford, were found guilty of high treason in the form of incest and plotting to kill the King.
Her indictment salaciously reads that she; "procured and incited her own natural brother...to violate her, alluring him with her tongue in the said George's mouth".

On 17th May, Anne and Henry's marriage was declared null.

On 19th May, she was beheaded.

On 20th May, the King was formally betrothed to Jane Seymour, and he wed her just ten days later.

Throughout it all, Anne maintained her innocence, swearing it on "peril of her soul's damnation". Much has been made of this declaration by some historians on the grounds of its seriousness given the strength of religion and belief at the time – others have pointed out that this was the lady who had just spent three years "married" to a divorced man – when the religion at the time was very clear that matrimony was a holy state entered into in the eyes of God and was a bond which could only be severed by death. Even today, historians are unable to definitively say whether Anne was guilty of any misbehaviour or not, especially since the main records of the trials have not survived.

Whatever the truth – it is entirely clear that the swiftness of the events unfolding and their culmination in the public beheading of a Queen left an indelible mark on the psyche of a nation: hardly surprising therefore to learn that legends of associated hauntings were left behind.

On the anniversary of her death every year, Anne herself is said to ride in a coach and horses down the main driveway of Blickling Hall in Norfolk, thought to be the place of her birth, carrying her severed head in her lap.

On the same night, her father, Thomas Boleyn, is said to be forced to forever pay penance for his part in the grisly story. He had worked hard to bring Anne to the favour of the King for his own political and financial gain, and of course the end result of that was the deaths of two of his children: Anne and her brother George. Thomas himself died in 1539.

His penance is that on every 19th May, his ghost must leave Blickling Hall at midnight in a coach drawn by four spectral horses (some versions claim both he and the horses are headless) and must travel to Wroxham, crossing 12 bridges over the River Bure before the cock crows. (In May, that would be somewhere around four in the morning).

Different sources give different lists of which bridges are involved, but in the main it seems to be Blickling, Aylsham, Burgh, Buxton, Hautbois, Coltishall, Meyton, Horstead, Belaugh, Oxnead, Braydeston and Wroxham. One obvious difficulty with this tale is that none of the bridges over the River Bure today are the same ones that were there in 1536... in fact not all of the roads will even be on the same route as would have been used back then. Not even Blickling Hall itself is the same – it was replaced in Jacobean times.

Nevertheless, I've researched what I can to see what, if anything, of these alleged hauntings remain, and such snippets as I could find are given below, bridge by bridge. If there was nothing other than the standard mention of poor Sir Thomas, I have not re-listed the bridge.

Blickling

Apparently Anne's poor brother George, Lord Rochford, also makes an appearance on this night, but his body is dragged by horses rather than afforded the comfort if a coach!

Hautbois

Nearby Hautbois Hall has a bricked up window which can be seen from the river. Legend has it that behind this is a room which was sealed up because of the very active poltergeist which resided there.

Coltishall

Nearby RAF Coltishall is haunted by a soldier from WWII.

Meyton (or Mayton)

This is one of the oldest bridges still standing – dating back to around 1630. Only one of its arches still spans the river, and this perhaps demonstrates how the course of the river has altered somewhat over the last few centuries.

Belaugh

There have been various spellings and iterations of the name of this hamlet over the centuries, but all seem to be based on a meaning of "dwelling place by the water". As well as the ghost of Sir Thomas once a year, it seems that every night, the ghost of one Richard Slater can be seen. In 1695, Richard, who was a servant at the local rectory, stole some money and jewels and hid them in the garden to be recovered later.

Unfortunately, when he returned in the night to recover his booty, he was surprised by the rector. In his haste to get away, he slipped and the weight of the ill-gotten gains dragged him to his death in the waters of the River Bure. His death is re-enacted by his ghost every night.

See also 24th August for another anniversary haunting on this rather unfortunate bridge.

Wroxham

Records show that a brick and stone bridge was built at Wroxham in 1576 to replace an earlier wooden bridge, and has been rebuilt again since. But that means for the first few decades of his penance, Sir Thomas was probably rattling his wheels over an old wooden structure here.

May 21st

The Wakefield Tower, Tower of London, London

The Tower of London was originally built by William the Conqueror in 1078 a.d. and must have been a very imposing symbol of the new reign.

It has many ghosts – many of them Royalty -and allegedly one of a bear. There is reportedly much paranormal activity around the whole site – some as recently as 2014.

The particular haunting attributed to May 21st is that of King Henry VI.

He ascended the throne when he was only eight months old, and so for many years the country was run by a regency in his name.

It is possible that this long period of political instability caused by having a child as King in name only, with other factions manoeuvring to hold the reins of power, contributed to how weak King Henry VI is depicted as being when he did finally take up his birth right fully.

The country became embroiled in what was later dubbed "The War of the Roses", which was fought between the noble houses of York and Lancaster and their various followers. King Henry VI was captured or had a nervous breakdown several times, and other contenders declared for the throne, or regencies stepped in.

Henry was captured for the last time in 1471, and his captors declared that on May 21st he "died from grief" after hearing that his son had fallen in one of the battles. King Edward IV was crowned on May 22nd.

Most historians now agree that he was actually murdered that night in the Wakefield Tower in the Tower of London, probably at the order of the Duke of Gloucester (who himself later became notorious as King Richard III for the presumed murderer of the Princes in the Tower and achieved fame later still as the skeleton discovered underneath a carpark in Leicester in 2012.)

King Henry's ghost is said to appear just before midnight on the anniversary each year and pace mournfully around the tower before fading away.

Colesmere, Shropshire

According to the Doomsday Book, there was a site at Colesmere listed as a manor. This particular ghost story however, says that there was a monastery there but one day a spring burst forth out of the ground and formed a pool which drowned the monastery. Another version of the tale claims that Oliver Cromwell caused the bell to be stripped from an old church at the spot, had the church razed to the ground, and threw the bells into the mere.

Either way, the legends claim that the bells can be heard ringing out from beneath the water on 21st May each year.

May 22nd

St Albans

May 22nd is a fateful date in the history of St Albans – and indeed for the whole country. On this date in 1455 the first battle of the War of the Roses was fought. King Henry VI had ascended the throne some years before as a mere babe in arms – and this created a power void which the various noble families vied to fill. When the King did finally pick up the reins himself, it did not ease the situation at all since he was thought to be a weak man prone to bouts of ill health and easily swayed by those around him.
In this first battle, the King was defeated by Richard Duke of York, and many soldiers lost their lives in the affray.
Since then, it was claimed that a house later built in this site, called rather appropriately Battlefield House, was haunted by the sounds of clashing swords and men crying out every anniversary of the battle.

The house has long since been demolished, but allegedly it stood on Chequers Street before being replaced by a row of shops.

In time, the shops were redeveloped into the Cross Keys Pub, which in its latter years was held by the Wetherspoons chain until early 2012, when it was sold to Heritage Inns before being sold again in 2013 and redeveloped into the Bill's Restaurant which stands there today.
It would be interesting to see if the sounds can still be heard in this modern day and age...

May 24th and 25th

Ditchling Beacon, East Sussex

As its name might suggest, Ditchling Beacon is the remains of an Iron Age hill fort, one of the largest in the area, and standing high on the Downs where warning fires would be lit when invaders advanced. Beacon sites are to be found throughout Britain, since in the days before any faster form of communication, what quicker way to communicate trouble than at the speed of light – from one hilltop to the next as each warning fire was lit in response to the sighting of approaching danger.

Legend has it that this particular site is haunted either by the sound of the Wild Hunt passing overhead, or the sound every year of a phantom army passing by... which for some unknown reason is accompanied by a foul stench. It seems to have been last reported in the early 1930s.
There is also a Black Shuck haunting the area – one of the famed spectral Black Dogs so popular in British folklore.

One visitor in December 2004 was driving up the road past the Beacon late one night on his way home, when his headlights picked out the figure of a man walking up the road wearing high boots, a long coat, and a wide brimmed hat.

As the driver passed the figure, he wondered what on earth someone was doing out walking alone in such a remote area on a cold winter's night. That led him to wonder if the chap had been driving somewhere but his car had perhaps broken down, leaving him stranded and with no option but to set off on foot to try and find help. The driver pulled his car up short, and watched the figure walking towards him from behind in the glow of his car's brake lights. At this point, he was still working on the perfectly reasonable assumption that this was a normal, live human being walking towards him.

As he wound the window down in preparation of offering help as soon as the man drew alongside, he suddenly noticed in the mirror that whilst he could clearly see the coat, scarf, and hat reflected in the brake light glow, there was absolutely nothing where the face should have been.

He didn't wait.

May 25th

Offham Hill, Near Lewes, Sussex

On 19th May, 1264, Simon De Montfort's men defeated those of Lord Edward at a bloody battle which began early in the morning somewhere near Offham Hill, near Lewes in Sussex, with an estimated loss of some 3000 lives.

The story goes that horse riders or dog walkers out at around 7.30 in the morning on 25th May each year can hear the sounds of clashing steel, cries of men, and whinnying of horses.

The discrepancy in dates is usually attributed to the change from the Julian calendar to the Gregorian calendar since then.

Curiously – the other anniversary ghosts reported around the country from dates preceding the change in calendars seem to prefer to stick to the date as it is known, other than the date as it would be now. But I'll leave the pondering as to why that might be so to you. I will just mention that most sources say the Julian calendar is 13 days behind the modern day Gregorian calendar, which would presumably have put the anniversary on the day we happen to call 27th May…

Also of note is the fact that there is the remains of a causewayed enclosure from Neolithic times on Offham Hill (which will probably have remained in defensive use for considerable time through the ages) – is it possible its a much early clash people are hearing the echoes of?

St Benets Abbey, Ludham, Norfolk

St Benet's Abbey was founded on the earlier site of a 9th century monastery, and is said to be the site originally of where a holy man named Suneman the hermit was martyred by the Danes.

At the time of the Norman Conquest in the 11th Century, King Harold instructed the then Abbott, Aefwold, to defend the coast along this part of the country against invasion. At this time, the abbey was a very rich holding, with 28 churches within its domain, and would have been a significant part of the local landscape and social infrastructure.It is from this time that the cyclical haunting is said to spring.

The tale goes that on that fateful day in May, the Normans were laying siege to the Abbey.
One of the monks, ironically named Brother Veritas (the Latin for truth), perhaps motivated by equal measures of a desire to reduce bloodshed and a desire for self-advancement, secretly approached the Norman encampment and struck a deal with them.

He agreed to open the gates and allow them to enter in return for their solemn promise that there would be no further killings, and also a guarantee that afterwards they would make Brother Veritas the Abbott.

At the agreed time the Normans stormed the abbey, and were able to defeat it since the gate was duly opened to allow them access.

However, they failed to keep their word and immediately put every monk they could find to death by the sword, showing no mercy whatsoever. Once the horrible deed was done, they hauled out Brother Veritas to witness what his perfidiousness had wrought, and ceremoniously crowned him Abbott of his ruined Abbey and dead comrades. They then promptly hung him from the walls of the bell tower of what was for a few fleeting moments "his" abbey. To this day, on the anniversary of the event, it is claimed that screams can be heard emanating from the within the ruins, and sometimes a faint shadow can be seen moving on the bell tower walls.

A second ghost also haunts the ruins. It is said that one of the monks, Brother Pacificus (the Latin for "peace") happened to have been away when the slaughter occurred, and he returned to the abbey to find all his brethren murdered. In sorrow he stayed living there alone like a hermit until he died some years later – but even now sometimes the figure of a monk with a small dog as his companion can be seen rowing a boat silently through the early morning mists or walking near the abbey.

In the early 1990's a boat crew taking part in the Three Rivers race in their punt were returning past St Benets in the small hours of the morning, when they spotted a small boat ahead of them in the mists. Whilst trying to angle their tack so as to avoid a collision, at least two of the crew saw the boat and heard its oars. When they drew level however, it had disappeared completely, even though there was nowhere for it to have disappeared to.

One of the crew was so puzzled he went back and checked in broad daylight – and confirmed for himself that there was simply no way the boat could just have disappeared from view at that spot. The Three Rivers Race usually takes part on the first Saturday in June each year.

Some sources also claim that sometimes, on a summers evening, the abbey can be glimpsed from the river as if still in its former glory – seen for just moment with its walls intact and pennants proudly flying from its tower. Yet another source claims there is a tunnel between the nearby church, the other side of the River Bure, and the abbey, in which there is concealed large amounts of treasure guarded by a spectral black hound.

In April 2011, the Out There paranormal team conducted an investigation at the site, and you can watch their clip about it on YouTube. They measured some slight fluctuations in EMF and two investigators thought they saw some shadow movement.

May 27th

Tower Green, Tower of London, London

The Tower of London appears again with another yearly manifestation – and this one relates to another truly shameful incident in the bloody history of the building.

In 1541, King Henry VIII was busy proclaiming himself as the head of the Church of England – in effect denying that the Holy Pope in Rome was the head of the Church. This scandalised many of the great and good of the day, but few were brave enough to speak out against the despotic King.

One who did dare to speak out and declare that this latest act was wrong was Cardinal Pole – but he was wise enough to say it from the safety of France, far away from the vengeful clutches of the King.

Unfortunately the Cardinal's 67 year old mother Lady Margaret Pole, Countess of Salisbury, still resided in England, and the King had her brought to Tower Green for execution on charges of treason.

When told to kneel at the block, she defiantly answered, "So should traitors do, and I am none", before belying her age by trying to sprint away from the executioner. He proceeded to chase the poor old woman around Tower Green, literally hacking her to death in front of the horrified witnesses.

Not surprisingly given its gory horror and the highly wrought emotions it must have evoked in the watching crowds, this scene or parts of it are said to re-enact on that fateful day each year.

The only actual sighting I could find though, was one visitor to the Tower on 27th May 2013 who felt someone unseen tap on their shoulder. Perhaps the Countess was trying to warn them to keep their head and shoulders intact...

May 28th

Sutherland House, Southwold, Suffolk

Sutherland House is now an award winning seafood restaurant and hotel, but was once a grand house in the town.

The story goes that Admiral Edward Montagu, the First Earl of Sandwich, stayed here on the eve of the Battle of Sole Bay.

Whilst he here dallied with a red headed serving wench, but when he failed to return from the battle the next day he left her bereft, and her ghost can sometimes be seen gazing forlornly from an upstairs window waiting for the return of her lover.

Doors often open and shut by themselves on this day, and disembodied footsteps are heard.

In real life, the Earl was married and presumably was on reasonable terms with his wife, as the couple had ten children together. This doesn't of course preclude the possibility that he also had a mistress or two. He was also a friend of Samuel Pepys, and it is documented that the Earl was tired of the war and felt very morose about having to go to battle yet again – for some reason he was sure he would not be returning alive.

Sadly, his fears were to become an actuality as his body was washed up on the shore after the battle, and the charred remains were only recognisable as him because of the clothing he wore.

May 29th

Southery, Norfolk

Southery is a small village in Cambridgeshire. It only has a little over a 1,000 residents according to the 2011 census, but it does have an interesting little legend. It is said that on 29th May every year, if you are unlucky you might hear the howling of the Southery wolfhound. If you do, you will die within the year.

The legend says that when the area was still surrounded by fens, there were wild clans roaming within them which would frequently attack the small settlement and its little enclave of resident monks.

Eventually, the locals took to using ferocious Wolfhounds to protect the village, but when times grew harsh and it was difficult to finds enough food to give to the ravenous dogs, they became feral and learned to feast on decaying human flesh.

Finally, since there was not enough food to sustain a whole pack, only one huge dog was left, and he was seen as the protector of the village. When the new church was built, the Bishop of Norfolk came to the village to hold a feast on that date in order to officially open the new church.

Unfortunately one of the soldiers send along to guard him caught sight of the huge dog and went to slay it with his sword – thinking it a dangerous wild animal. The dog retaliated by tearing his throat out – and was shot full of arrows for its trouble.

Ever since then, he has given his mournful cry on the anniversary of his death each year.

May 30th

St Mary and St Walstan's Church, Bawburgh Norfolk

The church is named in honour of St Walston, who died on May 30th 1016 and is buried there. Every year the church commemorates the event, but in 2016 they held a number of events in honour of the one thousand years anniversary.

St Walstan was said to have been born into a high ranking family in the area, but at age 12 decided to forsake his privileged lifestyle and go and live instead as a humble, impoverished, yet pious farmworker.

He remained true to his chosen lifestyle throughout his life, and would freely give away clothing and food whenever he could. He would pray for the sick or the dying, and even over sick animals that people often brought to him. He was respected and revered for his piety and generosity in his lifetime.

He died on 30th May whilst scything a field, and in accordance with his wishes his body was laid in a cart drawn by oxen to be taken for burial.

When the oxen stopped for a brief rest, a holy well sprung up miraculously out of the ground, and so the good man was eventually canonised by the Church. The church was built and dedicated to him, and ever since pilgrims have made their way to the site to revere him at both the church and the well.

It is said that on every anniversary of his death, strange blue lights can be seen dancing over the well and the churchyard. Historically, there are numerous documented accounts of miraculous healings taking place of both people and animals, with the most recent I could find being in 1928 when its waters were said to have cured a horse from terrible sores which would otherwise have resulted in the beast being slaughtered. However, the addition of the blue lights to the tale seems to be more recent - and yet without any actually cited incidents.

May 31st

Potter Heigham Bridge, Norfolk

Potter Heigham is a delightful village on the Norfolk Broads and is swamped with tourists every year. It really does seem to have an unusually large number of ghosts associated with it for such a small location.

This particular legend claims that sometime in the 1700s Lady Carew wished to advance her social position and financial security by securing the marriage between her daughter and the wealthy bachelor Sir Godfrey Haslitt of Bastwick, for her daughter Evelyn.

She engaged a witch to help her bring her plot to fruition, and accordingly the witch created a potent love potion, but would not accept any monetary payment. Instead she made Lady Carew swear that if the potion worked, whatever the witch asked for would be granted. As in all good cautionary tales,

Lady Carew agreed without being sensible enough to check exactly what the price would be.

The potion was covertly slipped to Sir Godfrey in his drink, and it must have worked its evil magic since he fell in love with Evelyn and the pair married on 31st May 1741. Following the lavish wedding in Norwich the bridal party return to Bastwick for the reception, but on the stroke of midnight the party was interrupted by the doors bursting open. A skeleton rushed in, kidnapped the new bride and carried her away in a coach drawn by four black horses.

The wedding party bravely gave chase but as the coach reached Potter Heigham bridge it burst into flames before tumbling over the bridge's parapet and into the water below, with Lady Evelyn still inside. The witch had collected her grim price.

It is now said that on the night of the 31st May you can hear the sound of horses' hooves and the screech of the wheels until a fiery coach appears over the bridge before plunging into the water.

There don't seem to be any actual sightings of this spectral coach, however.

St James Palace, Marlborough Road, London

St James Palace, one of the royal residences in the capital, boasts more than one ghost story, but we are particularly interested in the one pertaining to 31st May. Unlike many other stories in this book, this particular tale has a much more recent origin.

In the early hours of the morning on this day in 1810, the household was roused by a commotion and screams from the bedroom of Ernest Augustus, Duke of Cumberland. His valet was the first on the scene and found the Duke bloodied but alive, and his regimental sabre, covered in blood, lying by his bedroom door.

As the doctor came and started treating the Duke's wounds, others went to seek out the second valet, one Joseph Sellis. To their horror they found Sellis lying on his bed with his head almost severed from his body.

An inquest concluded – somewhat bizarrely – that for reasons unknown the valet had attacked his master, then returned to his own room and committed suicide. Quite how one could commit suicide by almost chopping off one's own head, yet leaving the murder weapon in another room, is somewhat beyond my comprehension.

I'm not the only one who finds this tale as an explanation a little, shall we say, tall?
Court gossip and talk of a cover up was rife after the affair ended, with all sorts of theories being put forward as to the "why", but most agreeing that the "how" was poor Sellis being murdered on the orders of the Duke or by the Duke, and then the Duke faking the attack on his own person to cover the matter up. Since there were many other scandals attached to the Duke during his long lifetime, anything is possible.

Either way, the result is that on the anniversary of that fateful night, the ghost of the valet can be seen walking the corridors with a ghastly gash across his neck.

Hill Hall, Theydon Bois, Essex

Hill Hall was built in 1560, during the reign of Queen Elisabeth I. Two rare wall paintings from the 16th century still survive within its confines, and although it is now subdivided into private residences, it is owned by National heritage and can be visited by prior arrangement on the first Wednesday of the month at certain times of year.

I have only been able to find one very scant reference to its annual haunting, so am a little sceptical as to the validity, but supposedly on 31st May each year a phantom coach and horses clatters down its driveway. The account says the coach is mustard coloured, but gives no reason for its annual appearance.

There is reference to the place being haunted in the 1940s by an unspecified presence in one of the bedrooms, and again in the early 1970s by a white-clad female figure in the grounds. While still a manor house, it was said to be haunted by a large back dog who would lie across the beds: perhaps it was this spook who made its presence known again in the 1940s?

Chapter 6 – June

The Kings Arms, Rotherfield, Sussex

Although the Kings Arms, which was in a converted seventeenth century barn, seems to have ceased trading as a pub, it was once known to be haunted through June by the ghost of a young girl, who would tug on people's clothes, or was sometimes seen as just a pair of bare feet running along the corridors.

There was one review of the pub in 2011 which described "horrible locals" staring at you as you ate, and the landlord and landlady drunk and obnoxious...it doesn't sound like it was the most salubrious if places when it was open! The pub was listed for sale in 2012, and seems to have faded from view since then. Perhaps its new owners could shed more light on whether or not the ghost still runs down the corridors.

June 1st

Hickling Broad, Norfolk

Hickling Broad makes another appearance – it certainly seems to have more than its fair share of spooky happenings!

Allegedly on this night each year, a female voice can be heard singing gently and the sound carries across the broad. There doesn't seem to be any tale as to why this might be but it is possible it is linked to another ghostly tale for the area – the woman in white who can sometimes be seen punting silently through the mists from one side of the broad to the other.

There was an Augustinian Priory here been 1185 and 1536 a.d. – one can't help but wonder if there is a connection there.

Wistow's Grave, Leicestershire

This is an interesting tale, as no-one can be 100% sure of its actual location!

The story is this. In 839 a.d. the King of Mercia, King Wiglaf, died. Unfortunately his heir, Wistan, was too young to ascend the throne immediately, and so the King's brother Behrtwulf took the throne. Wistan had not renounced his birthright, so theoretically Behrtwulf should just have been a Regent.

However, in 849, some ten years later, Wistan was a young man and starting to look ready to take up his responsibilities. Behrtwulf's son, Brifardus, knew that if Wistan were out of the picture, then he himself would stand to inherit the throne. He tried at first to marry Wistan's mother, but Wistan forbade it.

The devious cousin then called together a council and meeting at a certain place, and at this meeting he took up his sword and struck Wistan a might blow to the head, stoving in his skull.

However, Wistan was a devout Christian, and it is said that the heavens were so angry at the foul deed that a pillar of light shone forth where the body fell, reaching far up into the heavens, and that this pillar of light remained for all to see for the next 30 days.

Thereafter, the skeletal remains of Wistan proved to be impervious to fire, and at other times through the years were seen to sweat as if still mortal.

A church was built over the spot where Wistan was murdered, and he was duly canonised and became St Wistan.

Every year, on the anniversary of his death, it was claimed that human hair could be seen sprouting from the ground where he fell for an hour or two before mysteriously disappearing.

Curiously both Wistow in Leicestershire and Wistanstowe in Shropshire have at times claimed to be the site of the foul deed. Although it seems most historians have come down in favour of it being St Wistans church at Wistow in Leicestershire, the truth is that records from so long ago are unclear, inaccurate, or just plain missing – and when you add in the many place name changes over the centuries – you begin to see the problem.

I can't find any records of anyone in recent centuries claiming to have seen the hair, but if you visit *hauntingsofengland.com* and look for their investigation of Wistow Church from 16.10.15 it makes quite interesting (if somewhat cheesy in places) viewing. They captured some strange sounds, and several EVPs – Electronic Voice Phenomena. One of these is a voice which seems to say "you killed me – give me some rope".

Curiously one of the investigators can be heard saying that there is "a stone around here somewhere" which on certain nights if the year bleeds – as it was used to "smash in the head of some prince". Since Wistan's skull was indeed crushed, I wonder if this is another version of the same legend which is known more locally.

June 2nd

Soham Railway Station, Cambridgeshire

This next tale is a far more modern haunting than we usually find as anniversary ghosts.

On 2nd June 1944 a munitions train was pulling into Soham when the leading carriage caught fire. Had the whole train caught alight, with the massive arsenal of explosives it was transporting, the result would have been apocryphal.

The quick thinking driver and fireman on the train, realising they could not put the fire out safely, detached the carriage from the rest of the train and pulled it as far clear as they could before it exploded. The resulting explosion took out windows all around, and cost the lives of the signalman, Frank Bridges, and the fireman, James Nightall.

James Nightall and Benjamin Gimbert, the driver, were both awarded the George Cross for their quick thinking and selfless bravery.

Since then, on the anniversary, it is claimed that the explosion can still sometimes be heard. To be fair, though – I couldn't find any records of anyone actually hearing it.

Newtyle, Angus, Scotland

Newtyle is a small village just a few miles north of Dundee in Scotland.

Supposedly, on the 2nd June each year there is a (possibly) headless ghost dressed in white who wanders the area of Bulb Road, which makes an eerie groaning sound as it moves.

Unfortunately, I have only been able to find one source for this data, and no further detail as to why it might occur. Nor do there seem to be any records of an actual sighting.

June 11th

Old White Lion, Haworth, Yorkshire

This story relates to the very strange death of Lily Cove, in 1906. Lily was a 21 year old, vivacious daredevil, who performed by jumping from hot air balloons and parachuting to earth at Galas and village shows – to the amazement of the crowd below. At this point in history, anything that flew was still a huge novelty and most ordinary folk would never have seen a hot air balloon or a plane.

Lily would be seated on a small trapeze below the tethered hot air balloon which would rise majestically into the air, and a mechanism was rigged in such a way that when she jumped from the balloon after gaining sufficient altitude, it would automatically trigger the release of her parachute.

This fateful day was to be her seventh such jump. She was supposed to make the jump on Saturday 9th June at the Gala itself, but on that day despite repeated attempts, the balloon simply refused to rise – possibly due to the heavy atmospheric conditions on that day. Lily agreed to make the jump on the Monday evening, supposedly to avoid disappointing the crowds – perhaps back then the sheer novelty of such a performance would be enough to attract the crowds back?

In any case, the attempt was made at 7.40pm on Monday 11th June. Lily rose into the air seated demurely on her little platform below the balloon, and waved to the crowd as she rose to a height of around 700 feet.

The balloon was of course drifting slightly in the breeze and was being followed by a pony and trap who would retrieve Lily after her feat of bravery. As the balloon rose, Lily was seen to make the jump and the parachute opened as intended.

However, one observer later testified that he clearly saw Lily shrug her shoulders free of her parachute harness when still about 100 feet from the ground, and fall to her death from there.

The first three people on the scene testified that Lily was breathing when they reached her, but that she died due to her extensive injuries within minutes.

Her body was rushed back to Room 7 at the Old White Horse Inn, where she had been staying over the weekend. No-one will ever know why she deliberately freed herself from her parachute – since no reason for apparent suicide was ever given. Some have speculated that the parachute was drifting towards the local reservoir, and that Lily was terrified of water and may have detached herself rather than risk being caught in her chute and drowning in the cold waters.

Since that sad day, Lily's ghost is said to haunt the Old white Lion, particularly room 7 where she was laid to rest and where she spent her last few days alive.

It is said that sometimes guests are awakened by the sight of her standing at the foot of their bed. Some have even said that they are awakened with a jolt and the sensation of falling dizzily. I did find one travel writer who stayed in Room 7 for three consecutive nights in 2010, but nothing untoward happened.

Interestingly, a lot of the accounts I found gave the date of the haunting as 10th June – but Lily definitely died on 11th.

June 13th

Horsey Mere, Norfolk

Horsey Mere is one of the Broads (or lakes) in Norfolk. The legend is that in Roman times, children were buried in the lake by tying a weight to their little bodies to take them to the bottom. Since then, on June 13th each year, they can been seen flitting around the lake as they are allowed to run and play again for one hour on this mortal world.

Another version I found says it was the Anglo Saxons who buried their children in the Mere in this way.

In truth, the Romans did not afford their normal burial rites and customs to children below a certain very young age. Small children who died below this age were referred to as **"arpagi"** and were neither cremated nor formally buried in family plots.

It is possible to conceive of them using weights in the water to dispose of bodies if in fact they were in this area, but there is no historical reference to this that I can find.
Nor can I find any convincing accounts of anyone witnessing this paranormal phenomena at Horsey Mere.

June 14th

Goodrich Castle, Herefordshire

Goodrich Castle is a medieval castle near Goodrich in Herefordshire and is open to the public via English Heritage. If visiting as a disabled visitor, it's worth asking at the kiosk as you can avoid the long walk up to the castle by driving the car up there to two disabled parking bays at the top. It is a stunning location and well worth a visit.

During the English Civil War the castle was a Royalist stronghold, and was under siege in June 1646. Legend says that Alice Birch, the daughter of the Parliamentarian who was attacking the castle, and her Royalist beau, Charles Clifford were amongst those holed up within its walls. When it became apparent that the fortress might not withstand the siege, the two lovers mounted Charles' horse and attempted to flee since they knew that their clandestine affair would mean they would be shown no mercy, but the weather had been poor and the River Wye was swollen and flooded. When they tried to cross, the lovers and their horse were swept away to their deaths.

Legend says that their ghosts can be seen on the ramparts of the Castle on the anniversary - or on stormy nights they can be seen urging their terrified horse into the river.

I found an interesting EVP clip (look under *www.wynott.com castle ghosts* if you want to hear it). It is not linked to this legend, and the clip was taken in August 2010, so no direct link there either, but the film was being taken from a boat on the Wye just below Goodrich Castle.

The edit claims the eerie voice captured is saying "He's found it" but to me it could equally sound like "We drowned here" or maybe even "surrounded". See what you think.

There are quite a few photos to be found on the web of mysterious looking misty shapes within the dungeon area of the castle (which has its own legend of the ghost of an Irish Chieftain once imprisoned here).

The Falcon Hotel, Castle Ashby, Northamptonshire

The Falcon Hotel at Castle Ashby was originally built in around 1590.

The legend goes that on the Eve of that Battle of Naseby, the Parliamentarian forces gathering for the fight stopped at the forge here and entreated the blacksmith, a man named Arthur, to re-shoe some of their horses. Being loyal to his master, a Royalist, he refused, and so on the morning of the battle they hung him from the walnut tree in his garden.

The battle was fought on 14th June 1645, and so the date must also the anniversary of poor Arthur's death. Allegedly, he still moves objects around in the hotel.

In 2010 Northants Haunted conducted an investigation at the site and posted their video on You tube.

Their medium picked up on a blacksmith being present who was hung because he didn't finish a piece of work, and they also had a session of Ouija board and table tipping that you can watch.

Maidstone Road, Sevenoaks, Kent

The story goes that on 14th June each year, Maidstone Road in Sevenoaks Kent is haunted by the ghost of an old lady who was killed here whilst crossing the road in 1959.

Most sources describe her as white haired and wearing a fawn coloured coat. One source added that she wears a pleated skirt and red shoes. Apparently, she steps out in front of cars who screech to a stop thinking they have hit her – and sometimes find another car also stopped on the other side of the road who thinks the same thing, when clearly she could not have stepped off both kerbs at once.

Some reports describe it as the junction where the A21 and the A25 cross – but if this is the case, then that part of the road is actually called Westerham Road... not Maidstone Road. I could not find any historical mention of a fatal collision here.

Nor could I find any accounts of anyone actually seeing this particular ghost – but there was a driver in 2009 who saw **two** figures step out in front of his car somewhere along this general stretch of road, who then promptly disappeared right in front of him.

Naseby Battle Site, Northamptonshire

The English Civil war took a decisive turn in favour of the Parliamentarian side at the infamous Battle of Naseby on 14th June 1645. Some historians have estimated that over 6000 troops died that day – and that in total the Civil War wiped out 5% of the English population at the time.

For some years after the war, it was said that people returning to the site would watch a spectral re-enactment of the battle. This faded away over the years and now occasional figures are seen stumbling through the dark looking weary and battle worn, or else the sound of cannon fire is faintly heard.

In 1949 a young couple cycled out to the area for a picnic, and in broad daylight saw a heavy horse drawn waggon with bone weary, bedraggled men wearing leather jerkins and high boots stumbling alongside it which vanished before their eyes.

In 2008 the Northampton Paranormal Society conducted an investigation at the site, and captured a photograph which was published in the Daily Telegraph on 12/7/08 which they believe shows a man in armour carrying something and walking along through the dark.

In Sep 2016 another paranormal group conducted an investigation at a site close to the battlefield known as the Slaughter Fields, where allegedly those fleeing the conflict were captured and put to the sword. You can watch the video of their investigation on line at www.hauntingsofengland.com – and see what you think of the several EVPs they captured.

It certainly seems very likely that the site is still very active in a paranormal sense.

June 15th

Hitchin Priory, Hitchin, Hertfordshire

Hitchin Priory was originally a Carmelite Monastery built in around 1317a.d. Over the years it changed hands and was rebuilt, and the present day structure is a beautiful building set in acres of rolling parkland which is often used as a wedding venue or to host conferences.

It might be a slightly braver bride, however, who chooses to get married there on 15th June. This is the night when it is claimed the headless ghost of a Cavalier called Goring can be seen riding desperately towards the Priory, trying to reach sanctuary and his sweetheart.

It is said that this is a re-enactment of his final moments, for having been flushed out of hiding at HighDown House in Pirton near Hitchin during the Civil War (possibly after the Battle of Naseby the day before), he was captured within sight of the priory and beheaded on the spot. Unbeknownst to him, his lady love witnessed the brutal slaying from the upstairs of the priory and collapsed in horror – dying a few days later from shock. One account says she saw him from Highdown House.

In 1911 Ellen Pollard, who was then the owner of Highdown, presented a paper to the Archaeological Society detailing how he was seen riding a white palfrey (a name for a docile horse normally reserved for ladies to ride) towards Hitchin Priory every year on 15th June. Curiously though, some records claim his death as being 8th July 1644.

Certainly the priory seems to be very active from a paranormal point of view. In 1973 a group of schoolboys staying there witnessed a misty figure float in their room, and in 1980 a night caretaker doing his rounds saw the ghost of a lady wearing a short sleeved blouse hovering at the top of the staircase. He refused to ever go there unaccompanied again.

On another occasion a security guard saw a room full of men playing cards, but when he called for back-up they had mysteriously disappeared. Yet another saw a coach and horses pull up outside the back door of the priory, only to promptly fade away right before his frightened eyes.

You can see the video of a ghost hunt on line from 27th October 2016 which claims to show an orb morphing into a pair of transparent legs. It seems very likely from the stories that you need not be there on just the one night of the year if you want to witness something of the paranormal.

Cley Hill, Wiltshire

See 15th March for the full entry.

June 19th

Lochlee, Glen Esk, Angus, Scotland

I have been unable to find anything but the very barest of details on this manifestation – and all sources I could find repeat the same few sentences.

There was once a renowned piper living in Glen Esk, but he was whisked away by the faeries to play in their realm, and mortal ears are only allowed to hear the haunting beauty of his music once a year, emanating around the waters of Lochlee in Glen Esk.

Perhaps in today's busy world, the sound is lost or people hearing it just assume it is sound carrying from someone else's stereo.

June 20th

Cadbury Castle, Somerset

Cadbury Castle is an Iron Age hill fort in Somerset, which has long held associations with claims that it is also the site of the legendary city of King Arthur – Camelot. The earliest of such mentions came in 1542 from the writer John Leland, who wrote, *"at the very south end of the church of South Cadbury standeth Camallate, sometime a famous town or castle..."*

Certainly archaeological digs in the 1960s proved that there had once been a massively fortified site on top of the hill dating back to the 6th century a.d. – which would coincide with the presumed era of King Arthur.

There are various versions of the legends here: but all relate to either 20th June (Midsummer's Eve) or Christmas Eve (associated with the winter solstice). It is clear the legends have intertwined and merged over time with the celtic festivals of renewal for these two auspicious times of year.

On this night, it is variously claimed that King Arthur can be seen striding around the hill, or riding with a company of his knights down the oldest lane coming from the hill, or riding to the holy well at nearby Sutton Montis Church to water their horses, or even once every seven years riding out to feed their horses.

In 1986 one ghost hunter kept a vigil up there but encountered nothing, but a second ghost hunter attempting the same vigil in 1987 believed he heard the sound of a flute coming clearly from the woods below the hill in the middle of the night.

On 23rd June 1995 another witness encountered a man on horseback wearing what looked like armour, who rounded a corner just ahead of them. When he hurried to the corner to look there was no sign of the rider, and nowhere he could have gone.

Eastwell Park and Manor, Ashford, Kent

The original manor was built in 1540 for Sir Thomas Moyle. Apparently one of the bricklayers at the time was thought to be an illegitimate son of King Richard III.

The building has undergone many rebuilds since then, but it is actually the grounds which interest us.

Apparently, on 20th June every year, the ghost of a horseman can be seen galloping up the driveway towards the manor, but veers off course and vanishes just before hitting the lake.

One story I found claimed that the history of this was that it was a dispatch rider, who was riding in haste in thick fog. He mistakenly veered off course due to the weather, and he and his horse crashed headlong into the lake at speed – drowning the pair of them.

One ghost hunter has loaded pictures of "orbs" taken over the lake at night onto the popular social media site Pinterest. Personally, I think it's just insects caught by a digital camera.

Bossiney Mound, Bossiney, Cornwall

Bossiney Mound is a very strange little hump on the landscape – clearly manmade and thought to be the basis of a motte and bailey castle.

Although not a ghost, this story is included here just out of curiosity. Apparently at midnight on Midsummer's Eve every year, the incredible Round Table of King Arthur, supposedly buried beneath the mound, rises briefly to the surface and illuminates the sky with a brief flash of light. It waits for a moment to see if the King has returned, before sinking back out of sight.

Souther Fell, Cumbria

Souther Fell lies in the northern part of the Lake District, and unsurprisingly, for the area, is steep and cragged.

And yet, very surprisingly, in 1735, 1737, 1743 and 1745 a.d. witnesses saw what they thought was a spectral army passing along the top of the ridge. On the last occasion, even carts were seen amongst the soldiers – and there was no possible way for a cart to be on top of that virtually inaccessible ridge. It is claimed that on the last occasion, 24 credible witnesses saw the spectacle, and the next day they made an expedition up the ridge to find as expected, no trace whatsoever of cart nor man nor beast – and no humanly possible way for them to have been up there.

There is also a much earlier account from nearby in the Lake District, from 1513 a.d, when a witness saw something very similar even though there were no troops in the area at the time.

Purse Caundle Manor, Purse Caundle, Dorset

This wonderfully named manor house dates from 1470, but there was supposedly an even older building on the site prior to that. This older building was a hunting lodge for King John, and was apparently where the sick and injured hunting hounds were cared for by John Aleyn until he himself died in 1293 a.d.

It is perhaps from this period that the legend began – of a pack of baying hounds or "shucks" which haunt the area on Midsummer's Eve, before being called back to heel by one shrill blast on a hunting horn. Some versions of the story say that they can also be heard on New Year's Eve.

June 21st

West Kennet Long Barrow, Near Avebury, Witshire

Sitting close to Silbury Hill and not far from the famous stone circle at Avebury, West Kennett Long Barrow is believed to have originally stood with its front entrance open to the elements, and aligned in such a way that the dawn sun would have illuminated the interior.

Eventually, and possibly as long ago as 4,000 years, it was filled up with chalk and stones and its entrance sealed with huge Saracen stones. It is possible that this deliberate closure happened at the same time that Avebury was being built.

It had clearly been used as a burial mound, since when excavated some 46 skeletons were found within it. There may well have been more originally, since at least one account from the mid-1700s tells of a local doctor who would dig up the bones and ground them into a powder for his "medicines".

Every year, at dawn on Midsummer's Day, a man in white robes with a large white dog standing by his side can be observed standing on top of the mound. They wait there patiently until the first sunlight breaks the horizon, then turn and walk into the mound itself. If he can still be seen even today, then he is possibly the longest-serving ghost in the country.

At least one source claims they appear on 24th June, not Midsummer's Day.

Other paranormal happenings are credited to the site. In 1992 one female tourist was grabbed by the arm as she explored inside the barrow, and something unseen tried to drag her deeper inside.

Others have reported hearing whispered voices, the faint sound of chanting, seeing a ball of light or a black mist, and experiencing feelings of dread when inside.
In April 2007 one ghost hunting team heard a female voice and footsteps, and two distinct knocks emanating from deeper inside the mound.

Nan Clark's Lane, Mill Hill, London

Nan Clark's Lane is in North West London, and is a leafy lane which leads to some fields and woods, popular with dog walkers.

The tale goes that the local tavern, now called the Rising Sun, once had a popular and pleasant barmaid working there called Nan Clark.

Unfortunately, she had a very jealous husband, who one day came storming into the pub already drunk, and began cursing at his wife and accusing her of having an affair.
As she tried to protest her innocence, he dragged her out of the hostelry and down the lane in front of horrified onlookers, and then drowned her in the small lake found there. I can't help but wonder why the onlookers didn't step in to help the poor woman escape her untimely death.

Ever since, on the anniversary of her death, her ghost can be seen in the lane which eventually was named after her.
One local homeowner claimed to have taken a photo whilst hosting a Halloween party in her garden, and stated that it showed a mysterious old lady in the background wearing a high necked black dress and bonnet. It doesn't sound much like the description of Nan – but who knows.

Others claim that cars are known to mysteriously malfunction when being driven down the lane, and still others say mysterious balls of light are sometimes seen down there.

Bickleigh, Devon

Bickleigh is a very picturesque little village in Devon, situated along a steep sided valley at the bottom of which lies the River Esk. The river is spanned by an old stone bridge – this particular incarnation was built in 1809 – but there were other, older bridges before this one.

The story is that sometime in the 14th century, (possibly 1322 a.d.) one Alexander Cruwys, a local dignitary, met a rival from the Carew family on the bridge, and a sword fight ensued. The Carew man was slain and his body tumbled into the waters of the River Esk below.

Although Alexander was convicted of the murder and sentenced to death, he was rich enough to buy himself out of the sentence.

The story seems to have first been set in print in 1699. Certainly records show that there was an Alexander Cruwys at the time – his father was also Alexander and died the year before the alleged incident. The younger Alexander would have been about 35 at the time of the incident if it is true, and records show his date of death as 1333.

I haven't been able to find any accounts of actually seeing the ghost though – so one wonders if it was in reality a tale made up in the 1600s and just often repeated since.

June 24th

Blythburgh, Suffolk

The tale of the ghost of Blythburgh, a small village in Suffolk located along the marshy coast, is fascinating and gruesome.

The story is that motorists on the B1125 Blythburgh to Westleton Rd sometimes see a girl in a blue dress dart across the road – and promptly disappear.

She is thought to be the ghost of one Anne Blakemore, who was raped and murdered on the spot in 1750.

This is where the story gets really interesting.

Anne Blakemore really did die in 1750, and her supposed killer was sentenced to death.

The case was reported in the Derby Mercury on 14th September 1750. An army regiment was stationed around Blythburgh, partly to combat the smugglers which were using that part of the coast. Attached to the regiment was a black drummer called Tobias Gill, known as Black Tob. He was described in the paper as being "a very drunken profligate fellow".

On the night of 24th June 1750, he left the local hostelry in his customary drunken state. The following morning, he was found asleep in the fields nearby, lying next to the corpse of the hapless Anne Blakemore. The paper reported that he was said to have followed her and put a lewd proposition to her, and when she refused, he used her own handkerchief to strangle her and then raped her as she died.

He was arrested, tried, and convicted, despite his repeated protestations that he had not touched the girl. The judge sentenced him to death by "hanging in chains" – also known as gibbeting. This had only been made legal a few years prior, and was a truly terribly death.

Tobias was bound with iron bands forming a sort of cage round his body, so that he was kept in an upright position, and then the contraption was hung from the gibbet post. And there he was left, unable to move, and unable to find a swift death from the slow torture of dying of thirst and exposure over a period of time.

It was said that Tobias was so terrified at the prospect of his fate, unsurprisingly, that he begged the authorities to tie a rope to his neck and drag him behind the mail coach. His request was refused.

After his inevitable, and unenviably prolonged death, people became more and more restless about his fate – especially once rumours began to surface that actually, the coroner had found no marks or harm inflicted upon Anne's body at all...

Perhaps the two were secretly courting, and perhaps they both fell into a drunken stupor, but Anne succumbed to the cold that night and expired, or perhaps Black Tob did attack her or follow her or frighten her so that she died – we will never know the truth.

Either way, his ghost has repeatedly roamed the area ever since, so that it is now called "Toby's Walks", and Anne runs across the road, frightening motorists even in this modern age.

Even more curiously, I couldn't find a single report from modern times of anyone actually seeing either ghost... but I did find a report of a lorry driver driving long the nearby A12 in the 1970's and seeing a cart and horse being driven by a man and with a woman walking along side. He feared his lorry had clipped the cart as he passed them on the narrow road. He stopped his vehicle and went back to see what damage he might have caused and to check everyone was alright, but to his absolute horror there was nothing to be found: there was literally no trace of the horse, or the cart, or the people. There was nowhere they could have turned off or gone out of his sight.

Also at Blythburgh was the story of the Black Shuck who terrorised the local church many centuries ago and left claw marks in its door after killing two of the congregation.

Curiously, in May 2014 the papers reported that the skeleton of a seven foot long huge male dog had been uncovered at nearby Leiston Abbey during an archaeological dig.

When alive, the animal would have weighed in the region of 14 stone – a truly huge dog. The archaelogists were able to show that its bones dated back to roughly the same time of the tales of Back Shuck...

Oulton Broad, Suffolk

Oulton Broad in Suffolk is now incredibly popular as part of the Norfolk Broads boating holiday destinations.
Allegedly, in 1851, the owners of a cargo wherry (a type of sailing boat historically used in the Norfolk Broads with a distinctive wedge shaped sail), charged their skipper, Captain Stevenson, with taking a large sum of money down to Great Yarmouth. They wanted it taken by river to keep it safer than it would be on the roads, where highwaymen and footpads patrolled.

A large chest was supposedly loaded on board, and accompanied by the owner's daughter Millicent, who pretended that the chest was containing clothes for her to go and visit her Aunt in Great Yarmouth for a prolonged stay. They hoped by this ruse not to attract any unwanted attention to the true nature of their valuable cargo.

Captain Stevenson grew greedy at the thought of what he had on board. As they slipped towards Gt Yarmouth in the middle of the night, he killed his First Mate and heaved the body overboard, then went below hoping to avail himself of the charms of young Millicent and planning to kidnap her and make off with the money across the open sea.

Millicent however fought back, and rushed out onto deck screaming and wounded. The second mate tried to intervene, but the burly Captain struck him an almighty fatal blow and threw his corpse overboard. As he was thus distracted, Millicent seized her chance and stabbed the Captain straight through the heart – then herself collapsed and died from her wounds and shock.

The cabin boy, Bert, did not know how to sail a Wherry at sea on his own, so he untied the dinghy and set himself adrift in it. He was later rescued, and that is how the tale of what happened came to be known.

Since then, allegedly, on every 24th June at 12.30 am, the Mayfly can be seen enveloped in an eerie mist, struggling to make it across the broad and home with two spectral figures engaged in combat on board.

However, it is very likely that this entire story, which seems to have passed into Norfolk folklore, is a compete fabrication by Sampson "Ghosts of the Norfolk Broads".

M.W.Burgess, writing in issue 38 of the Lantern, has exhaustively researched the entire tale and concluded that none of the characters ever existed, it wouldn't be possible for a Wherry to make the journey described in Sampson's books in the timescales given, and there never was a Wherry named Mayfly....

And to put the final nail in the coffin of this tale, one blog response in 2011 tells how they were manoeuvring their own modern day sailing ship down the broad, but in trying to cheat the tide were staying close to the shore, whispering silently in the mist past holidaymaker's boats moored up for the night... only to have the papers report that terrified holidaymakers thought they had seen the Mayfly go past the night before.

Brundall, Norfolk

Perhaps not surprisingly given the location, as far as I can ascertain, this story also originally stems from the pen of Charles Sampson in his book , "Ghosts of the Norfolk Broads" since every iteration of the tale I can find all relate back to that one source. He claimed that on this night in June and again on 18th September, the ghost of the Bishop of Brundall sails down the river past Brundall on a barge covered in fine silks and rowed by 28 men. Anyone seeing the sight is blessed.

As far as I can tell, there is no such office as Bishop of Brundall – the nearest is the Bishop of Norfolk or the Bishop of East Anglia. This and the fact that there seems to be only one source for this story lead me to think that Mr Sampson was rather fond of spinning ghost tales and passing them off as real – and inordinately fond of ascertaining a particular date to his tales!

As an aside though, I did find one blog writer who claimed to have been moored on the river at Brundall when very late one night, after they had already been asleep a couple of hours, they were suddenly awoken by their boat rocking and swaying in the wake of something large passing them.

Annoyed at someone being so inconsiderate, they opened the hatch (which was directly above their bed) and poked their head out to glare at the miscreant – only to find the river silent and still, with the moonlight shining across it unbroken by even the slightest ripple. Their experience was in November though, so perhaps there is no correlation whatsoever.

West Kennet Long Barrow, Near Avebury, Wiltshire

See the entry for 21st June.

June 27th

St Mary's Church, Beaminster, Somerset

This is a curious little ghost story – which also perhaps is more fiction than fact...

It was allegedly first related in the Gentleman's magazine in 1774, and told of a haunting from some fifty years prior, in 1728.

Supposedly, at that time, one John Daniel died as a young boy, and was interred at the local church. As was the custom in those days, the very same church was also used as the school house. Some seven weeks after the burial, on 27th June 1728, some of the school lads were playing outside.

Hearing some strange noises from within the church itself, they went in to investigate. Five of them witnessed a coffin laying on one of the pews, and sitting nearby the figure of a young boy, hunched over as if writing. One of the lads suddenly exclaimed that he recognised the figure - it was none other than his recently deceased half-brother John, and in the way of young lads everywhere, he helpfully threw a stone at the apparition.

As a result of the sighting, and having become suspicious as to the cause of death, the local dignitaries ordered the exhumation of the body, and after some deliberation and deposition of witnesses, determined that his death had not been caused by him having a fit whilst out alone playing in the fields, as his mother had testified, but was actually by strangulation.

Despite this, no attempt was ever made to bring his murderer to justice.

A later writer, Roger Gutteridge (2009) determined that the real mother was Hannah, who died in 1714. His father was Isaac Daniels, who remarried to a lady called Elisabeth in February 1718, and soon fathered a second son to her.

When Isaac died in 1726 he left land and money to both his sons, and the assumption is of course that Elizabeth killed, or caused to be killed, her step-son John in order to secure everything for herself and her own son.

Roger Gutteridge goes on to tell of a local cowman, who entered the field behind the church in August 1998 at around 4.45am, in order to check on one of his cows who was calving. Turning on his powerful torch in order to locate the beast, he was shocked when the beam picked out the form of a woman and child standing looking at the cow. When the beam hit her, the woman turned to look at him and was seen to have pink eyes. The pair then turned and walked towards the gate into the church yard.

However in total contrast to this history, Rupert Willoughby, an actual descendant of the Daniels family, wrote an historical article on some of their history in 2011.

James Daniel was born 1615 and died 1711 aged 96. He took part in the Battle of Sedgemoor in 1685, when he would have been in his early 70s! His sons did not accompany him at the battle because they were not old enough.

One of his sons was called John, and fathered two boys, James and John: he cannot have been our ghost if he lived long enough to father children. James became a Coroner, and John a surgeon.

John Daniels, the younger grandson and later surgeon, was born in 1717. His mother was called Hannah, and she remarried to one Thomas Bosher. He would seem to fit the biography of our ghost, since had he but died in 1728, he would have been around 10 years old (a young boy of school age), who probably did have a step-sibling if his mother remarried.

Unfortunately for our story though, John lived a full and prosperous life, finally dying in 1781 having married and fathered children of his own.

Even more curiously, although Rupert Willoughby *does* write about a later ghost story associated with one of his female ancestors, he remains silent on the subject of any ghost called John. This suggests that if there were any spark of authenticity to the ghost story relating to John, Rupert would quite likely have included it as well as the later ghost story.

It therefore seems likely then that the original account was, quite simply, fictional but using some historical names for apparent authenticity.

Chapter 7 - July

July 1st

St Bartholomew Church, Smithfield, London

St Bartholomew's Church in Smithfield, London, boasts the title of second oldest church in the capital.

It was founded in 1123 a.d. by one Rahere, a monk, or canon, or jester, or musician (depending on which story you read!) of the court of Henry I. Supposedly, whilst still a young man, Rahere made a pilgrimage to Rome, but unfortunately became very ill whilst there. He had a vision during his illness, and from that vowed to persuade the King to allow him to build a church which would be dedicated to St Bartholomew and which could care for the poor, the sick and the elderly.

The King granted him land and permission to build, and it is believed the church opened its doors in around 1127 or so. It continued to be built on and expanded for some years to come though, and Rahere became its first Canon.

The church continued to provide healing and solace for some 400 years, and was also the inspiration for the founding of St Bartholomew's Hospital in the reign of Henry VIII. It also witnessed a lot of horror in it time: William Wallace was hung drawn and quartered in front of it (remember the film Braveheart?), Wat Tyler was murdered close to it, and hundreds of heretics were also executed in front of it.

Some sources claim that the ghost of Rahere still haunts his beloved church, and that at 7am on the morning of July 1st every year he can be seen standing by the altar or emerging from the vestry.

Unfortunately, I can't find any listing of what the import of the date is. Various sources list his death as 1143, 1144 or 1145 a.d., but no one of them give the actual date or cause.

Supposedly, as well as Rahere, the sounds of screams and the crackle of bonfires can also be heard at any time of year in the church, and a shapeless mass is sometimes seen to float down the aisle – emanating a feeling of pure evil as it passes.

In 2001, the Evening Standard reported that the motion sensor alarm was triggered in the middle of the night, and when the incumbent went to investigate and turn it off he heard the sound of footsteps even though no-one else was in the building at the time. The following day the alarm company checked the equipment for faults, and was puzzled to find that only the motion sensor next to Rahere's tomb had been triggered – none of the others.

In 2008, Haunted Earth posted a YouTube video of an investigation at the church with several EVP's highlighted – you can find it under "London's Most haunted Church – Halloween Special". In it they mention that one priest was allegedly burned to death in an iron cage outside the church.

In 2015, one visitor wrote that she sensed something evil in one part of the church which made her feel very uncomfortable. It would seem therefore, that paranormal activity is still a possible factor even today.

July 2nd

Marston Moor, Long Marston, Yorkshire

On July 1st 1644 Prince Rupert broke the siege of York during the English Civil War, and liberated the Marquess of Newcastle. Perhaps feeling confident following his success, on the following day he engaged with the Parliamentarian forces near Long Marston, led by Lord Fairfax and the Earl of Manchester.

The battle didn't start until 7pm – and a thunderstorm struck whilst it was raging. By 10pm that night it was all over – and over 4000 of Prince Rupert's men lay dead in one of the bloodiest and most decisive battles of the whole conflict. Parliamentarian losses are estimated as much smaller – possibly less than 500 men – but either way that's around 25 men dying every minute for three solid hours. Is it any wonder that this horrific day left a psychic imprint on the surrounding landscape?

The casualties were buried in mass graves in unconsecrated grounds, and it was a prevalent belief at the time that the dead would not lie quietly in their graves if not given proper funeral rites.

The first reports of the ghosts seem to be in the form of some very fancifully worded pamphlets printed in 1659 – and the reports of hauntings go on even to this day.

In 1932 some men driving across the moor in a car saw their headlights pick out the forms of three men walking along wearing what was later confirmed as Cavalier uniform. As they neared the group, the men suddenly disappeared from view.

Bewildered, the witnesses stopped their car and searched for the men, but nothing could be found.

The ghostly figures were seen again in 1968 by a group of tourists trying to find the right road to Wetherby. They assumed they had seen a group of half a dozen re-enactment actors walking along the roadside until it was pointed out that they were actually crossing the site of the battle itself...at night.

During the 1970's, one writer lived in a farmhouse on the edge of the battle site, parts of which dated back to the right period.

Throughout her childhood, the sound of men screaming and the clash of armour was a "normal" evening sound which she became so accustomed to that she would pay little attention to it. She described how the sounds could be heard all year round, but became even more noticeably active around the anniversary of the battle each year.

In 1992 drivers once again reported seeing bedraggled, weary looking soldiers walking along the roads.

So, if you are driving in that area at night, please take a camera with you. You may well be lucky enough to get a true ghost photograph.

July 3rd

Burgh Castle, Norfolk

For the main entry for this is see 27th April – but some witnesses claim that they saw the body of the messenger fall from the battlements on July 3rd.

July 4th

Lansdowne, Near Bath, Somerset

On July 5th 1643, the battle of Landsowne, part of the English Civil War, was fought in this area. The cavalry of the royalists suffered heavily.

There seems to be very little detail on this tale, and no recent records, but allegedly on the evening before the battle, the sound of madly galloping hooves can be heard.

I have been unable to find any records of actual witness testimony.

July 5th

Whitley Beaumont Tower, Mirsfield, Near Dewsbury, Yorkshire

This folly or summer house which was built in 1752 is all that remains standing of the fine manor house belonging to the Beaumont family which used to be sited here.

The legend is that one member of the family, Richard Beaumont, was nicknamed Black Dick of the North, and was a ne'er do well of the area who was variously believed to be a highwayman, or gambler, or a bad debtor. Legends say that he got a young servant girl pregnant and then murdered her, and that he died as a result of a duel. It is said that his headless ghost will appear at midnight every year at the folly which became known as "Black Dick's Tower" on 5th July.

Unfortunately, the historical facts don't really match up. Richard Beaumont was first cousin to Queen Elisabeth I, and was knighted by James I in 1609.

In 1610, he founded the Kirkheaton Grammar School, and in 1615 he was Justice of the Peace for the County of York. In 1625 he served as Member of Parliament for Pontefract, and in 1628 he was made Baronet of Whitley by Charles I.

It seems highly unlikely he would have had any need to turn to highway robbery, although he could feasibly still have been a gambler and have bad debts. It is said that James I gave him the nickname of Black Dick of the North, and that this was just because of his swarthy complexion and his very dark hair.

More damningly for the legend, he did not die on July 5th but on October 20th, and the Tower was not built for another hundred years after his death!

It is just possible that there was a highwayman roaming this area, and over the years the legends have become twisted, because Black Dick does sound rather like the name of a highwayman.

Certainly in 1982 two young lads out playing with their sled in the December snow saw a man on a horse watching them. He was wearing a Tudor clothing, and something about the sight of him felt "off" and scared them so much that they ran off. The next day when they returned, their sked marks were clearly visible in the snow, but no sign of any hoof prints. Their sighting was at Thornhill Edge, which is around four miles from the Tower as the crow flies.

Perhaps the ghost of an actual highwayman does in fact roam this area and has just become romanticised over time?

In July 2013 the Paranormal Encounters Group held a vigil at the Tower, and their medium allegedly picked up on a number of names including Richard Beaumont. More interestingly they also captured the sound of a cackling laugh on their recorders, and some misty shapes in their photographs. You can watch their investigation on YouTube.

July 5th and 6th

Sedgemoor, Near Bridgwater, Somerset

The Battle of Sedgemoor was fought on 6th July 1685, and was the last ever battle fought on English soil. It was the final battle of the Monmouth Rebellion, and some 800 Monmouth supporters were captured and sent to the assizes for trial, after which they either suffered hanging or deportation. The trials were presided over by Lord Chief Justice George Jeffreys, and became known as the Bloody Assizes for the complete lack of mercy shown to the prisoners. It is also known that Judge Jeffreys extorted money from many of the prisoners.

One particular village in West Dorset, a small hamlet then called Corscombe, had 12 of its men hung for their part in the rebellion, and they were then dismembered and their bodies boiled in pitch and then publicly exhibited as a warning to the rest of the village.

It is said that around the anniversary of the battle (which took place in the early dawn) the sound of horses galloping can be heard through the night, and disembodied voices call "Come Over" from across the River Carey. Sometimes, the clash of arms and the screams of men dying can be heard, and on other occasions strange lights have been reported over the site.

Another legend claims that when one rebel soldier was captured, he was offered his freedom if he could outrun a galloping horse. When he succeeded in performing the feat, the soldiers jeered and cut him down anyway, murdering him in front of his sweetheart. She was so distressed that she drowned herself in the river.

It is said that her ghost, a figure in white, can be seen gliding along the marsh by the river where her lover died.

One teenager who hitched a lift from a lady when crossing the area many years ago, knew nothing of the history of the moorland he was hitching across, but sensed and heard the sounds of battle all around him just before he was picked up. The kind lady driver who had stopped to pick him up, then explained to him about the Battle of Sedgemoor.

In the mid 1990's (although one source I found listed the date as 1944 – which is quite a discrepancy!) The Ghost Club once conducted an overnight investigation there. I have seen it variously listed taking place in either 1944 or in the 1990s – which seems an incredibly wide discrepancy.

At just after midnight they heard a dull banging sound, then about an hour later the ground beneath them shook and vibrated for a couple of minutes. Around 3.00am they heard what sounded like a woman's cry in the distance, and later still the sound of drum beats a long way off and the beat of galloping hooves.

In July 2011 the Avon Paranormal team investigated the site, and picked up cold spots around the area of the monument. At one point in the small hours of the morning, one of the "cold spots" was felt to grip quite painfully onto one of the investigators' arms. Sudden localised drops in temperature are often attributed to a ghost trying to manifest itself.

The investigation team's sound equipment picked up distant shouts, loud grunting noises, the sound of a horse (even though none of the surrounding fields had horses in them), and someone gave a deep sigh in response to one of the investigators remarking to the other when chatting about the battle, "Do you think they were scared?"

In July 2015 two paranormal teams collaborated to investigate the site overnight, and brought a medium with them. You can watch their investigation on YouTube, uploaded in October 2015 under mystery.mag.com.

The medium picked up some general information and at one point they heard the sound of a gunshot. It's always possible it was a real gun shot of course – there is a fair bit of night shooting goes on around the English countryside, although a large proportion of that would be by air rifle, which is practically silent.

It seems very likely that the site is still worth a visit for paranormal activity.

July 6th

Ashdown House, Forest Row, East Grinstead, Sussex

Not to be confused with the Ashdown House in Oxfordshire (and previously Berkshire before the county borders were changed), Ashdown House in Surrey is actually a private boarding and day school, and as such is obviously not open to the public.

Supposedly on this day every year, the sound of footsteps can be heard going up the stairs inside the house. I have not been able to ascertain why or what the haunting relates to.

It also means that there are no recent stories of any haunting to be found – since the school itself was founded in 1843 and is understandably unlikely to want to scare the children there!

Road from Westonzoyland to Bridgewater, Somerset

Following the Battle of Sedgemoor detailed above, the defeated Duke of Monmouth fled the scene. He was soon captured, and was executed on July 15th.

It is claimed that as well as the skulking figure of Monmouth himself, this stretch of road (now the A372) is haunted by the faint sound of soldiers singing hymns. This is an eerie echo of how, centuries ago, the remains of Monmouth's defeated army tried to keep their spirits up by singing as they slowly returned to their homes.

Many of the unfortunate wretches who were pawns in a bigger political game were later rounded up and tried in what became known as the Bloody Assizes for the barbaric way in which many of the prisoners were treated.

July 7th

Glasshayes Mansion, Lyndhurst, Hampshire

The manor at Glasshayes was first mentioned in records in 1728, but our ghost comes from a much later period. The oldest part of the present building was constructed in the first decades of the 1800s by George Buck (whose wife is incidentally also sometimes seen as a ghost here, having died in the property in 1826).

The house was later bought by Richard Fitzgeorge de Stacpoole, a member of the French aristocracy and the First Duc de Stacpoole. He led quite a colourful life flitting between France and Italy, eventually abandoning his wife and children on the continent, and living here at Lyndhurst with his two friends, a married couple. Allegedly, he ran a successful smuggling operation from the house.

He died on 7th July 1848, and since then supposedly music can be heard on this date emanating from empty function rooms in the hotel. Legend claims that this is the Duc hosting his annual Ball for the Dead.

At other times, whenever the building has undergone renovation, it is said that his ghost appears as an old man seemingly angry at the changes being made.

A builder in the 1970s claims to have challenged what he thought was an eccentric old man trespassing on the site, who was claiming to be the Duc De Stacpoole in an irritated voice. Thinking he needed to escort the strange old gentleman with his wild claims from the property, the builder reached out to guide him away gently by the arm, only to have his hand and arm pass right through the gentleman. The builder, probably not surprisingly, fainted.

The hotel closed in 2015, and certainly in May 2017 was still an abandoned derelict of a building.

Knighton Gorges Manor, Isle of Wight

Another anniversary ghost said to plague the site of this once fine manor house (see also January 1st) is that of Sir Tristram Dillington, seen riding his horse on the anniversary of his death each year.

He allegedly committed suicide in 1721 after becoming addicted to gambling following the death of his wife and his four children who all succumbed to fever.

In order to hide the true cause of death (and thus incur an inquest and possible loss of the property since the law at the time said that the property of a suicide would pass to the Crown), it is said that his valet mounted his master on his horse, Thunderbolt, and then drove the terrified animal into the lake so that it drowned, carrying the corpse of its master.

Historically, Sir Tristram is recorded as having died "without issue" (e.g. without having surviving children) and that therefore his baronetcy died with him.

Another version of the tale says that he is seen driving in a coach and horses on the anniversary of his death, rather than riding the unfortunate horse itself.

Yet another version says that the horse was simply turned loose with his master's corpse on board, so that when the corpse fell it would simulate a riding accident.

Whatever the original truth of the story behind the haunting, it was apparently sporadically active from 1900 to 1975 at least, so may still be detectable today.

July 11th

Breydon Water, near Great Yarmouth, Norfolk

This story originates with our old friend Mr Sampson, and as such must be taken no doubt with a healthy pinch of salt. He claimed to have been on a fishing trip on Breydon, and to have seen a luminescent host of galleon style ships pass by in the night, heading towards Burgh Castle. He and his companion heard the men on board singing and talking, but as the sight passed by it gradually faded from view.

Perhaps unsurprisingly no-one else seems to have recorded the sight.

July 15th

Horton, Dorset

Following the Battle of Sedgemoor and his defeat (see earlier in July) the Duke of Monmouth fled south across England trying to escape to the continent.

He rode across Wiltshire and onto Cranbourne Chase – which then was a wilderness with very little in the way of human habitation.

Eventually he made it as far as Horton Heath on July 8th, where his luck ran out and he was captured, apparently trying to hide in a ditch beneath an ash tree. On 15th July he was beheaded at the Tower of London, and it was not an easy death as the executioner botched the job – taking 6 or 7 blows to sever Monmouth's head.

The exact location of the original ash tree is not really known, although the field there was for a long time called Monmouth's Close. (In English history, many fields were named, and a "close" was often one which was close to a habitation. Even today, many fields retain their ancient name, but it is often only the local farmers who know them).

It was said that on the anniversary of Monmouth's death, his ghost could be seen cowering in the ditch below the tree, trying eternally to evade capture.

The modern day site of the ash tree is believed to be near Slough Lane in Horton.

July 24th

Shooters Hill Road, Blackheath, London

The earliest written reference to this ghost seems to come from Elliott O'Donnell writing in 1932. He described the ghost of a lady dressed in white who could be seen wandering the area where Shooters Hill Road and Well Hall Road (now the South Circular) meet. Sometimes her forlorn cries could be heard, and he wrote of several witnesses who had either seen or heard her in the late 1890's.

It is claimed that a skeleton was unearthed in the area in 1844 which was that of a blonde haired woman who had evidently died from the blow of a blunt instrument to the head.

In 1881 an ancient pistol was found buried in the basement of the nearby Old Bull Hotel, and it was supposed that the butt of the pistol was likely the blunt instrument which was used to dispatch the young woman.

Curiously, in the same area on 18th July 1963, a man called David Beck driving through the area saw what he first thought was a large dog lying injured by the road.

When he stopped his car however, intending to try and help the poor creature, to his astonishment it got up and loped into the nearby woods. As it moved, he could see that it actually resembled a big cat far more than it did a dog.

Later the same day, two policeman on patrol were astonished when "a large gold coloured creature" jumped over the bonnet of their police car.

A hunt for the supposedly escaped big cat ensued, involving 126 policemen and also police dogs, but all their efforts resulted in naught but some huge paw prints almost seven inches across: big enough to belong to a lion or tiger.

Interestingly, the prints showed claw marks, which tend on the whole to be more likely found on a dog's prints than a big cats. One can't help but wonder about the possibility of a modern day Black Shuck.

July 27th

Killiecrankie, Scotland

The Battle of Killicrankie was fought during the first Jacobite uprising on 27th July 1689, between the Highlander forces supporting Kings James I and James VII and the lowland and English forces supporting William of Orange.

Although the Jacobites won the day, their losses were heavy and in particular they lost their leader, Bonnie Dundee.

It is claimed that on the anniversary of the battle each year, the sounds of fighting and men dying can be heard, and around 7pm in the evening the area can sometimes be seen bathed in an eerie red glow which stains even the grass red.

Sometimes the misty forms of highlanders running down the gorge can be glimpsed, and supposedly one woman enjoying a picnic on the grass beside the river looked up from her sandwiches to see a momentary glimpse of dead soldiers lying around her.

In a particularly creepy twist, one legend also claims that sometimes the ghost of a woman stealing valuables from the bodies of the dead and dying can be seen, but if she realises you are watching her beware, for she will chase after you and if she manages to touch you, death will follow within the year...

Chapter 8 - August

August 1st

Holy Trinity Church, Ingham, Norfolk

This curious little legend centres on this very ancient church in Ingham, in the Norfolk Broads.

The site dates back to at least the 13th Century, when there was a Priory Church here housing a college of Friars. Built and rebuilt many times over the years, there still remains inside some very ancient tombs and effigies. One is the tomb of Sir Roger de Bois, who died in 1300, and next to him his wife Margaret, who died in 1315.

There is also the effigy of Sir Oliver de Ingham, and his head is resting on the severed head of a Saracen. (This of course being the time of the Crusades).

The legend says that at midnight on 1st August each year, Sir Roger and Sir Oliver rise from their tombs, kneel and pray at the altar, and then make their way down to nearby Stalham Staithe where they fight a Saracen, toss his body into the water, and then return to the church to sink quietly back into their graves for another year. A staithe is a landing or dock area on a navigable stretch of water.

I have also seen versions which claim it is just Sir Oliver, and others where it is claimed they have a dog accompanying them. (One of the other tombs in the church – that of Sir Miles Stapleton who lies hand in hand with his wife Joan – does have a small dog carved on it which was named Jakke)

I have not been able to find any explanation behind the legend, nor any recent sightings.

There is also supposed to have been a secret tunnel unearthed underneath the altar during restorations in the 1860s, which was believed to lead to the local Manor House, and in which were found 19 skeletons. The tunnel was allegedly sealed back up without further exploration.

Just outside the wall of the church, a "tall, pale lady" is also said to haunt, and there is also a ghostly monk – see the entry for Christmas Eve.

August 2nd

The Rufus Stone, Minstead, New Forest, Hampshire

Not far from Canterton in the New Forest, set a short walk away from the main A31, stands the Rufus Stone.

The version standing today was laid in 1841, and is coated with metal to preserve it from the elements. The metal is inscribed with the story.

The stone (which replaced an earlier one laid in 1745) claims to mark the spot where King William II was fatally wounded and died. He was said to be out hunting with a party of his men and courtiers, when one of his men, Sir Walter Tyrrell, fired his arrow at a deer but he missed his target. The arrow, swinging wide, ricocheted off a nearby oak tree, and struck the King in the chest, killing him on the spot.

Supposedly, his men simply rode off and left his body there, and it fell to some local countrymen to load his body onto a simple cart and drag it to Winchester. Here, the unfortunate King was buried without the usual pomp and splendour afforded to the funerary rites of a monarch, and within three days his brother Henry had claimed the crown.

Sir Walter himself, afraid of retribution, is said to have fled to his native France.

Since then, it is claimed that every August 2nd, on the anniversary of the King's death, his ghost rise and walks to Winchester, following the route of his ignoble passage to his burial.

Certainly during his life the King was very unpopular – he was nicknamed Rufus for his ruddy appearance and red hair (hence the name of the stone) and was known to be a callous and merciless ruler towards his subjects.

Historians consider it possible that this was actually a deliberate regicide: especially given how his entourage simply rode off and left him. It seems highly unlikely as a natural reaction to a hunting accident, however unpopular the victim may have been, and one which would be guaranteed to cast aspersions of guilt.

There is also dispute as to where the actual deed took place. The earliest record of marking the spot seems to come from Charles II's reign (late 1600's), when the King visited the area and was shown the oak tree.

That would have been over 500 years since the deed, but given the longevity of English Oak trees it is entirely possible that the same tree would have been standing. Although the tree itself was cut down a hundred or so years later, the stone was erected to mark the spot. Historians however, think it was possible that the actual incident took place some miles away, nearer to Beaulieu.

In modern times, the sound of horses' hooves and the rumble of a cart's wheels have been recorded here, and one investigator visiting the site in December 2016 caught some light anomalies with her camera.

Castle Malwood, Minstead, New Forest, Hampshire.

After killing the King, as mentioned above, Sir Walter Tyrrell fled to France, fearing for his safety. On his way, he fled down what became known as Tyrrell's Lane in Burley, and stopped at Castle Malwood, where he washed the blood from his hands in the pond. Every anniversary, the pond is said to turn blood red in commemoration of his awful deed.

In actual fact, the names are getting mixed up with the passage of time in this telling of the story.

The true Castle Malwood is actually the name of an Iron Age hill fort nearby, but the King kept a hunting lodge in the forest which was named after the castle and called Malwood Keep. The party would have left for their hunting that day from this Lodge.

However you look at it, if Sir Walter was fleeing for his life, in so much haste that he left the King's body lying where it was, it seems a little strange that he would go back to where they were staying that night to wash his hands before leaving for the coast!

August 4th or 5th

Barton Broad, Norfolk

The tale goes that in the time of the crusades, one knight returned home after a long trip away to be presented with a beautiful baby daughter by his wife. He did not believe the infant could possibly be his – so he insisted the child be sent away and raised elsewhere.

Years later, after another long absence, he again returned home and caught sight of a beautiful young woman whom he lusted after and tried to court. (One has to rather pity his long suffering wife in this tale!)

The young maiden however was not interested in the older, grizzled crusader, for she had a young suitor whom she already loved very much.

The tale says that the crusader was so enraged at being spurned, that he shot a crossbow at the young man, but the beautiful young girl flung herself in the path of the arrow to save her lover and deflected the blow at the cost of her own life.

Another version of the tale claims that the two lovers tried to escape her unwanted suitor across Barton Broad in a boat, but the crusader fired at them with a cross bolt. His aim was unfortunately true, and the cross bolt holed the boat below the water line and sank it, leaving the hapless lovers to drown in the cold waters.

Either way, the not very chivalrous knight soon after became aware that he had just murdered his own daughter and was horrified. It's a shame he could not have been horrified at the thought of murdering someone else's daughter.

Since then, it is claimed that her beautiful face can be glimpsed in the early morning mists on either 4th or 5th August (depending which version you read). It is even claimed that the face, sometimes huge in dimension, can even be glimpsed from low flying aircraft.

August 11th

Beeleigh Abbey, Malden, Essex

Beeleigh Abbey, near Malden in Essex, is today a beautiful, partially half-timbered private residence which only occasionally opens its gardens for public viewing.

Originally built in 1190 a.d. as a monastery for the White Canons, it has gone through many iterations in its long history and it is not surprising it should have picked up a ghostly tale or two.

The particular tale of most interest for this book is that of its cyclical haunting – quoted by some sources as 11th August and others as 22nd.

On that day, one can seemingly hear moans and wails coming from the walls and from a particular bedroom which is believed to have been the master bedroom for a former owner, Sir John Gates.

Sir John was arrested and tried for his role in the plot to put Lady Jane Seymour on the throne of England in 1553, and was beheaded at the Tower of London. It is widely reported that the moaning is his ghost, bewailing his fate.

Only a small amount of research, however, throws up some questions about this tale: and the questions are summed up well by authors Christina Schumacher and Ron Bowers in their book "A gift from spirit – land of the wee folk".

Sir John was arrested on 21, July 1553, tried on 19th July, and beheaded on 22nd August. He was arrested in Cambridgeshire, and beheaded in London. Why then would his spirit be at Beeleigh Abbey at all?

True, he did once own the property, but he had already sold it in 1546 to one William Marche – seven years prior to his death.

Christina and Ron postulate the theory that the wailing might actually come from a set of ghostly monks who are sometimes seen outside the property, and who allegedly died when their escape tunnel, which they were hurrying down during the reign of King Henry VIII and the Dissolution of the Monasteries, collapsed and killed them all.

Their book includes an interesting photograph possibly showing a ghostly monk on the outskirts of the property.

Other accounts claim that there is poltergeist activity in the form of violently shaking beds and doors opening within the abbey itself, and one lady who stayed there reported waking in the morning to find teeth marks in her shoulder and hand.

St Mary and All Saints Church, Fotheringay, Northamptonshire

The reported cyclical ghost here is actually a sound – that of funeral music with trumpets and drums.

Richard, Third Duke of York and his son Edmund were both buried here on 30th July 1476 as a re-internment back in their home soil following their deaths some years earlier at the Battle of Wakefield, with all the appropriate pomp and ceremony due for men of their social standing.

The sound can sometimes still be heard on the anniversary – but the true anniversary taking into account the change from the Julian calendar to the Gregorian calendar in 1582.

The last record I can find of it being heard was by a schoolteacher and his wife in 1976.

August 13th or 14th

Pilchard Inn, Burgh Island, Devon

Burgh Island lies opposite Bigbury on Sea in South Devon, and is separated from the mainland by a spit of sand which forms a tidal causeway.

Originally called St Michael's Island (not to be confused with St Michael's Mount further south), it changed its named to Borough Island which later corrupted to Burgh.

On the island is the ancient Inn called The Pilchard Inn, and which now belongs to the hotel next door. A small whitewashed-stone building, it was originally built in 1336, possibly to house travellers building or visiting the monastery that once stood here.

In the late 1700s it was the known haunt of a smuggler known as Tom Crocker, who plied his "trade" up and down the cost in these parts. Legend has it that on 14th August (some say 13th) his sins caught up with him in the dour form of the Revenue men, who shot him dead in the porch of the pub when trying to arrest him.

Other versions claim he was brought to justice and hanged for his crimes near to the pub.

Whatever the truth, long since lost in the mists of time, his ghost is said to haunt the outside of the pub and sometimes the foreshore every anniversary of his death.

I could only find one actual account of something possibly paranormal happening, and that was in May 2005 rather than August.

A lady visiting the pub went to step into the garden to have a cigarette, but struggled for a moment to push open the door. As she did, someone gave her a hearty shove from behind, causing her to stumble.

Turning round to confront what she assumed was her husband following her, she was astonished to see him still sitting in his seat, and the barman still behind the bar – with no-one else present in the room! The barman attributed the unkind act to Old Tom...

August 15th

Rock, Northumberland

A curious little tale this, with very little back history or evidence to go by. Supposedly, on 15th August every year, the anniversary of her husband Henry's death, one might encounter the ghost of Arabella Lawson.

She can be seen hurrying from South Charlton, where she had been staying with relatives, back to Rock Hall, around three miles distant, where her husband was staying with his brother. It is said that she awoke in the middle of the night with such a fearful premonition that something was wrong with her husband that she got up and immediately set off to go to be by his side – breaking into a run as her brother-in-law's home came into view.

Her premonition was right, for at the Hall she found her husband dying following a fall from his horse earlier in the day, and was able to sit with him for a last heartbroken farewell as he passed away in her arms moments after she arrived.

One writer claims that her ghost was seen in 1969 by a cyclist staying at Rock Hall when it was acting as a Youth Hostel. He saw her figure in grey glide across the lawn and disappear straight through one of the walls of the building.

The Hall is a private residence today, having spent around 30 years up until 2013 as a small private school until rising costs and falling pupil numbers forced it to close.

Historically, the only thing we can say for sure is that the Lawson family did own Rock Hall for a while many years ago.

But of Henry and Arabella in real life, I could find nothing.

August 17th

Chicksands Priory, Chicksands, Bedfordshire

There has been a priory on this site since at least 1086 a.d., when it was listed in the Doomsday Book. The priory passed into private ownership after the reign of King Henry VIII, whose lawyer produced a report as part of the Dissolution saying that the nuns at Chicksands were not following their vows of chastity since at least two of them were found to be pregnant!

The priory was then owned by the Osbourne family for over four hundred years, but from around 1936 it became a secret service station, before becoming an American Air Force base for some years: where locals lucky enough to wheedle a pass onto the base were able to go and enjoy everything American from fast food to bowling.

After another spell back in the hands of the British military, it passed into the ownership of Bedfordshire Borough council, and houses have been built across much of the grounds replacing the military housing which was there before.

The legend goes that a nun called Berta Rosaca (I've also seen it spelled Bertha Rosetta) was found to be pregnant by her lover – one of the monks. He was beheaded in front of her, and then she was walled up alive to die a slow death. Since then her ghost has haunted the grounds – some say just on 17th August, others on the 17th of every month, and still others claims that she walks in any month where a full moon coincides with the 17th.

There are many accounts of sightings during the middle part of the 1900s when the military lived on the base, but not many more recent that I could find. One paranormal group did investigate in December 2006, and one of the investigators briefly saw a figure dressed in either a long robe or a monk's habit glide across the corridor behind him – even though on one side of the corridor there was no doorway and therefore no obvious reason why the ghost should be crossing through the wall there.

August 21st

High Street, Reedham, Norfolk

There is a legend that on August 21st every year, you can see the ghost of "Old Man Bern" running for his life as he is pursued by Vikings down to the waters' edge, where he makes his escape.

The most commonly given version of this story is that Bern was a huntsman to King Edmund, but became insanely jealous when the King struck up a friendship with the Viking Chief, Ragnar Lothbrok, and preferred to go hunting with him instead.

Bern seized his chance whilst he and Ragnar were alone one night on a hunt, with only Ragnar's hunting hound as a witness. He killed the Viking and professed to know nothing as to what might have occurred when the body was discovered.

However, the faithful hound was determined to take revenge on his master's killer, and every evening he would sneak into the Great Hall as everyone gathered for the evening meal and sink his teeth into Bern, until eventually the hapless man was forced to confess his heinous crime. As punishment, some versions say he was cast adrift in a boat, others that he was chased and escaped in a boat.

Either way, the sons of Ragnar Lothbrok were understandably peeved at the treatment of their father, and attacked the settlement at Reedham, killing all who lived there, including the King.

Historically speaking, this gets a little confused though. There was a King Edmund, who was killed by Viking raiders in around 869 a.d and who later was immortalised as a Saint – and hence the Suffolk town of Bury St Edmunds.

There was also a Ragnar Lothbrok, but records about him don't really come into play until 300 years after Edmund's death, when Norse accounts record that Ivarr, son of Ragnar, ordered King Edmund to be slain.

The earliest English account comes from around 100 years after the events, and it names the Vikings involved as Ivar and Ubbi. An account from 300 years after the event names three sons of Ragnar – Ivar, Ubba and Beorn – or Bern.
It is not until nearly 400 years after the event that tales first introduce Bern as the king's huntsman.

In truth then, the ghost of Bern, if ever seen, could either be a murderous huntsman escaping after killing a Viking Chief, or a murderous Viking escaping after killing the King!

That there is paranormal activity in general around Reedham is likely, as I found several accounts of haunted buildings and houses when researching as well as a UFO sighting in 2016 – but no accounts of anyone actually seeing Old Man Bern – whoever he was.

Blickling Hall, Blickling, Norfolk

Blicking Hall makes yet another appearance in this book – but this time with a ghost from a later period.

After the Boleyn family house fell into ruin, a new house was built on the spot by Sir Henry Hobart, 1st Baronet, in 1616.

The house remained in the Hobart family, and another Sir Henry, the 4th Baronet, became our ghost.

He fought a duel with one Oliver Le Neve, on 20th August 1698, at nearby Cawston. The two fought with swords, and Sir Henry was fatally wounded. He was carried back to his home at Blickling Hall, where he died the next day.

The spot on Norwich Road in Cawston where the duel occurred is marked by a memorial known as the Duelling Stone, and legend says that the sounds of the sword fight can still be heard here on 20th or 21st August.

In Blickling Hall, Sir Henry died in the West Turret room, where his groans of pain as he lay dying can also still be heard. One of the warden's dogs in recent years steadfastly refused to enter the room, remaining always on the threshold snarling with his hackles raised.

Interestingly, a UFO was reported over Cawston in 2017.

August 22nd

Beeleigh Abbey, Malden, Essex
Please see the entry on August 11th for the full story, since it seems slightly more likely that the hunting is actually on that date, but some sources quote it as 22nd.

August 24th

Belaugh, Norfolk

This seems to be another ghost from the pen of Charles Sampson and his book of Ghosts of the Broads – and there seems to be little else to reference it. Take it then with a pinch of salt...

Every August 24th, after a spectacular sunset, the ghost of Lady Alys can be seen down by the water's edge, still calling for her Viking lover Olaf, who will come for her out of the swirling mists on his long boat...

I have not found any recorded sightings, nor any historical reference.

August 31st

Beccles, Norfolk
There is a legend that the town of Beccles was once so plagued by rats that the good townspeople paid three chancers handsomely to rid them of the pests.

The three men, unbeknownst to the populace, struck a bargain with three witches in order to gain the power to lure all the rats by playing musical instruments so they would follow them down to the River Waveney, where the rats all hurled themselves into the water and drowned. The men were never seen again, other than as three ghostly figures seen once every year down by the water's edge. There are definite strains of the Pied Piper here (pun entirely intended).

Some versions of the tale are even more lurid, with the men being consumed by fire as the flesh falls from their bones for signing a pact with the devil at the witches' cauldron, and with the townspeople being fully aware of how their infestation was being resolved.

Sadly, I have been unable to find any actual sightings of the ghosts.

Chapter 9 – September

St Botolph's church, Boston, Lincolnshire

St Botolph's Church in Boston is a truly beautiful piece of architecture with a stunning tiered tower. Why it should have earned itself the slightly sad sounding nickname of "The Boston Stump" seems incredible, but there it is.

There are two stories concerning possibly the same ghost, or possibly two different ones. Some versions say it can most often be seen on September nights – others say it is this specific night you need to be there.

The tower of the church is around 273 feet high, and can be seen for miles around from the flat fenlands surrounding this ancient town. It is from this that you can apparently glimpse the spectral form of a lady falling to her death – perhaps with a baby clutched in her arms.

One version says it is the ghost of Sarah Preston, who was unfaithful to her husband while he was away from home, and invited a sailor into her bed. From him she contracted the Black Plague, and the virus quickly spread, killing hundreds in the town. Aghast at what her perfidiousness had done, she ran to the church crying "pestilence!" and flung herself from the tower.

The second story is that if you run around the church tower three times, the ghost of the Grey Lady will appear and fling herself and her baby from the tower. She was said to be a young widow so distraught at losing her husband at a young age in this life that she resolved to become a family with him again in the next: but instead as a suicide is doomed to repeat her act in limbo for evermore.

Some versions have Sarah Preston also clutching a child as she jumps, so it is hard to tell where the edges of those two legends have blurred over time.

On one occasion in the middle part of the 20th Century, one of the church vergers was understandably terrified when he saw the ghostly Grey Lady walking down the aisle whilst he was working in the church.

In the 1990's the church organist was working alone in the church late at night recording his organ music. He was playing late at night in order to minimise extraneous sound on the delicate recording equipment he was using. However, on playing the taping he had just made back, he was horrified to hear the clear sounds of footsteps approaching, even though he knew for certain that he was alone in the church.

In January 2012, the local paper published a photograph of a strange light seen on the second balcony of the tower at night – which some thought looked to be in the form of a lady.

And curiously, the church tower was once found to be the culprit for a radar echo the RAF were picking up in relation to a UFO sighting which had been reported to them.

Grenadiers Pub, Wilton Row, Belgrave Square, London

The building, dating back to 1720, was originally used as an officer's mess for the First Royal Regiment of Foot Guards.

After the Battle of Waterloo in 1815, the Foot Guards changed their name to the First Grenadier Regiment of Foot Guards in honour of their bravery against the French Grenadiers.

In 1818, the building was licensed to become a public house called The Guardsman, and later changed its name to The Grenadier.

At some point when it still housed the officers, the story is that one young officer was caught cheating at cards. His comrades were so completely incensed at his lack of honour as a gentleman that they beat him so badly he later died.

It is thought that the death must have occurred in the month of September, for that is when all manner of supernatural and spooky activity really kicks in every year at the property. People have seen figures moving out of the corner of their eye, heard footsteps coming from empty rooms, and heard low moaning sounds and sighs from the cellars.

In 1982 a photographer caught the image of a young man's face in one of the windows by the restaurant area. As this was prior to the age of digital photography, he would have had to blow the image up in a using a photographic dark room, and in doing so he fully expected the "face" to become clearer as perhaps a trick of the light and shadow, or maybe vine leaves from outside the window. (This optical illusion, where an everyday object seems to our human eye to form a face, is known as pareidolia. The human brain is sort of pre-programmed to try and recognise faces, so it tries to resolve indeterminate shapes and patterns into facial features).

Instead, to the photographer's horror, the image he was studying became even more clearly an actual face. Curiously though, the window in question, although at normal height inside the pub, is actual around 12 feet off the ground outside the pub – so no-one could ever have been stood there...

In 1992 the head barman was having a quick cigarette break down by the entrance to the cellar, when the temperature around him suddenly plummeted noticeably, and the ashtray resting on the shelf by his head suddenly launched itself across the space, narrowly missing him and leaving him feeling understandably terrified.

On another evening, chairs in one of the rooms were suddenly all moved at a time when the barman knew himself to be alone in the property.

It seems quite likely the site is still active in terms of paranormal activity.

September 3rd

Brampton Bryan Park, near Ludlow, Hereford and Worcester

Brampton Bryan Park is what remains of an ancient deer park, lying just outside the village of Brampton Bryan. Listed as a site of Special Scientific Interest, it has been owned by the same family for over 700 years. Although not open to the public as such, all sort of events are held there, and it is very often used for filming historic or period pieces, due to its beautiful unspoilt nature.

During the time of Cromwell, the owner was Sir Edmund Harley. His family were treated quite harshly by Cromwell after they fell out with him over political issues. When Cromwell died on September 3rd 1658, there happened to be an unusually strong gale which swept across the country.

As it passed, it did considerable damage to the ancient old trees within the park: and the legend was born that the Devil swept through the park carrying Cromwell on his way to hell.

It is claimed that sometimes on the anniversary, the sound of his passage can be heard - still crashing through the park as an unexplained sound.

September 8th

Rainthorpe Hall, Tasburgh, Norfolk

Rainthorpe Hall is a stunning Grade I listed Elizabethan mansion, with many outstanding architectural period features, and which boasts as well rare 17th century leather wall coverings. The original building probably dated back earlier than 1400 a.d. but it was destroyed by fire in 1500 a.d. Interestingly it went on the market in 2012 for around £3,000,000.

It was also the childhood home of Amy Robsart, who was the wife of Robert Dudley, himself widely known for being the lover of Queen Elizabeth I. Amy and Robert certainly seemed to live apart and saw very little of each other, and some thought it was likely that the Queen would marry Robert if the chance ever arose.

On the fateful day in 1560, Amy was at Cumnor Place in Oxfordshire (a manor which has long since been demolished). Abingdon Fair was taking place that day, and although she was only 28 she was not feeling well enough to go, but insisted rather that her companions and maid servant all go, leaving her alone.

Later that day, she was found lying at the foot of the ornate twin staircase with two head wounds and her neck broken. The tragic news immediately became something of a scandal which rocked the corridors of power. People whispered that Robert had ordered his wife's demise in order to free the way for him to marry the Queen. There was in due course an inquest into the sorry affair, which, lacking any hard evidence to the contrary, recorded a verdict of death by misadventure.

Although that cleared Robert's name legally, he and Elizabeth never did marry since the whiff of scandal would have been severely damaging to her political position.

The actual medical records from the inquest were found in the National Archives in 2008, but they detail wounds which it could be argued were consistent with *either* misadventure (falling down the stairs) or being murdered (neck broken and placed at the stair foot, or pushed down them) or suicide (throwing herself down the stairs) and have therefore added nothing to shed light on the ancient mystery. It does seem a little odd that she had asked to be left alone that day, sending even her faithful maidservant away for a day out.

Since then it is said that Amy can be seen on the anniversary of her death meeting with a male form in the gardens of what had been her childhood home at Rainthorpe Hall, even though she died so many miles away. Perhaps she returns to relive an earlier memory when she and Robert were still happy, or perhaps the male form is not Robert at all...

Until the property was demolished, her ghost could also be seen at the foot of the stairs at Cumnor Place.

Sadly there don't seem to be any recent accounts of Amy's ghost.

Old Bawn Road, Tallaght, Dublin, Ireland

There used to be a magnificent house on the Old Bawn Road in Tallaght, not far from where it crosses the River Dodder.

Although the house itself might be long gone, curiously the - possibly very inaccurate - tale of its ghost still lingers on.

The tale is that on the anniversary of his death every September 8th, the ghost of Archdeacon William Bulkeley is carried in a coach pulled by six headless horses, accompanied by a fellow passenger and two footman, up what would have been the entrance to the Old Bawn House.

Legend says that if you try to look inside the coach, you will be dead within a year and a day.

The problem with this tale is that Wílliam Bulkeley did not die on September 8th – his father Lancelot did. It was William who built Old Bawn House in 1635, but Lancelot died in 1650 "at Tallaght" – so perhaps he was living with his son by then as he was in his eighty-second year.

Whoever it is within the coach – they don't seem to have made their presence known in any recent times that I can find.

September 12th

Baldoon Castle, Bladnoch, Dumfries and Galloway, Scotland

In August 1669, Janet Dalrymple was forced to marry Sir David Dunbar even though she loved another. The wedding party returned to Baldoon Castle after the wedding ceremony had concluded to enjoy the celebrations and feasting, and all seemed well until that night, when the couple retired to their chamber for their wedding night.

The story goes that shortly after they had retired, terrible screams were heard, and when the guests rushed upstairs and flung open the bedchamber door to find out what the awful commotion was about, they found Sir David badly wounded, and Janet cowering in a corner still wearing her wedding gown but covered in blood. Some versions of the story say she was already dead – others that she went mad that night and died on September 12th -within a month of the wedding.

Sir David refused to ever speak of the night, Janet was not capable of speaking about it, and so no-one ever found out what had actually happened.

Speculation ran rife that either Janet's lover was hiding in the chamber and attacked his rival: either being killed himself or fleeing afterwards, or Janet herself attacked her new husband.

No versions of the tale seem to mention the probably obvious – Sir David trying to force himself on his new wife to the detriment of both of them.

This is probably because this was long before any kind of women's rights became legal, and so it would not be considered unusual at all for a husband to make his advances whether they were welcomed or not.

Some have even claimed that is was the devil himself who came into the chamber and attacked them both.

Whatever the truth, supposedly on the anniversary of her death every year, Janet's forlorn spectre can be seen wandering what is now nothing but a few scant ruins, still dressed in her blood spattered wedding gown.

There don't seem to be any recent sightings of her, so perhaps she has finally found peace.

September 13th

Newark Castle, Selkirk, Scottish Borders

All that remains of Newark Castle today is a ruined tower and some walls. It stands in the Bowhill Country Park which is itself open to the public. Built in the early 1400's, its infamy stems from the events following the battle of Philiphaugh on Sep 13th 1645, during the War of the Three Kingdoms.

The Marquis of Montrose and his army was defeated at the battle, and the camp followers (wounded men, women and children) were rounded up and somewhere between 100 and 300 of them were taken to Newark.

There, no mercy was shown, and all of them were slaughtered like cattle by shot, or sword, or bludgeon. Others were taken to Glasgow or Selkirk and put to death there, and at least another 80 women and children were thrown into the river to drown.

In 1810 a great quantity of human bones was found buried under the field just outside the castle which is known as Slain Men's Lea, and it is quite possible that this is evidence that the tales of the slaughter were entirely true. A "Lea" is one of the old names for a field or meadow.

It is said that every year, the screams and cries of the massacre can still be heard around the castle.

St Mary's Church, Overton Drive, Wanstead, London

Built in 1787, St Mary's church in Wanstead boasts itself as one of the finest Georgian churches in the country, and is understandably proud of the fact that it is still using the original pews.

The tale is that whenever September 13th falls on a Friday (which is roughly every six or seven years – the last one being in 2013 and the next due in 2019), there can be seen the Grey Lady ghost, wandering the graveyard searching for her husband who left her widowed only a few short hours after they were married.

Unfortunately, I cannot find what the back story to this is – and nor can I find any recent sightings.

The only "ghost" there in recent times was earlier in 2017 when the actor Tom Hardy played his character James Delaney in "Taboo" returning to see the burial of his father... and the scenes were shot in the darkened, dry-ice-filled church.

September 14th

Breydon Water, Norfolk

There is a mention of a battle between a pirate ship and two smaller ships which can be seen on Breydon water every September 14th – but there seems to be very scant detail on it that I can find, and what there is looks like it may well source back to our friend Charles Sampson.

He writes a very fanciful story, supposedly told him by an eyewitness, of the three ships battling out in front of their very eyes on the night of September 14th. The "witness" claimed the spectacle lasted for a full half hour and was literally in full glorious technicolour.

I won't be rushing to Breydon Water expecting to see anything.

September 21st

Berkeley Castle, Berkeley, Gloucestershire

Incredibly, Berkeley Castle has been the home of the same family for some 900 years, and today can be visited by the public on afternoons from Sunday through Wednesday. It also plays host to special events which are listed on its website.

Perhaps the most notorious part of its incredible history is the imprisonment and death of King Edward II within its walls. King Edward II was thought of as a weak king, and there were problems throughout his reign, with political shenanigans going on, and strained relationships (to say the least) with the French and the Scottish.

Edward married Isabelle of France as part of the attempts to bring a lasting peace between England and France – but theirs does not seem to have been a happy union. For one, rumours have abounded ever since about the precise nature of his relationship with his favourite at court, Piers Gaveston, and for another, Queen Isabella openly began an affair with her lover Mortimer, and ultimately the two of them took the crown from Edward.

Gaveston was executed by the nobles just five years into Edward's twenty year reign, but popular history still assumes that his death was partially to do with that possible illicit love match between him and the King.

Edward himself was imprisoned in Berkeley Castle in January 1327 where he resigned his Kingdom on January 21st. His death was reported to his son, King Edward III, as having occurred on 21st September of the same year.

By the 1330's, rumours were already circulating that Edward had died a horrible death – being pinned to a bed whilst a red hot poker was thrust into his rectum via a funnel. When I was at school, we were told that this method was used to avoid any signs of misdeed being visible on the outside of his body: but it seems there could have been less foul ways of killing someone without showing much outward signs than this.

Since then, it has been claimed that the sound of his agonised screams still ring around the castle in the anniversary of the dreadful deed.

However, some historians consider that there is some evidence that actually, Edward II was secretly allowed to leave the castle and assume a new identity as William the Welshman. Most also agree that at best the supposed manner of his death is probably not true but was propaganda at the time spread by those who did not support Isabelle and Mortimer.

In 2007, on the 680th anniversary, the T.V. personality Richard Felix – from "Most Haunted" – spent the night in the cell in which Edward was imprisoned as part of a commercial ghost tour event at the castle. He reported that there was no activity or sound through the night.

September 23rd

The Strood, Mersea Island, Essex

The Strood is the name for the only road leading on and off Mersea Island. At certain times, when the high tide is high enough, it is flooded by the encroaching sea, stranding motorists on the island for a few hours until the tide turns again.

It is on this lonely stretch of road that the ghost of a Roman soldier is often seen. Sometimes a passing motorist will catch a fleeting glimpse of him in the car headlights, or sometimes a passer-by will catch the sound of marching feet. Allegedly there can occasionally be heard the clash of swords and cries of fighting men. This activity is said to ramp up around September 23rd, and continue on through some of the month of October.

It is certain that the Romans did in fact visit Mersea Island, since a burial mound excavated in 1912 showed Roman grave goods and construction.

In 2005 one particularly intrepid ghost hunter tried walking about on The Strood in the dark on a night where the wind was howling and rain was squalling in from the sea. Despite his efforts, he neither saw nor sensed anything and his equipment gave no results either. He did though, have the foresight to wear a High Visibility yellow jacket for his investigation, remarking that he wished to investigate ghosts, not become one!

September 29th

Sherborne Old Castle, Sherborne, Dorset

Now known as Sherborne Old Castle to differentiate it from the newer one which replaced it, this beautiful old building dates back to the twelfth century, when it was built by Bishop Roger of Sarum. For some four hundred years it remained an ecclesiastical holding, but then Sir Walter Raleigh set eyes on it and persuaded Queen Elizabeth I to award it to him in recognition of his services to the country.

In January 1592 he was granted a 99 year lease on it by the Queen. However, she had not at the time realised that he had secretly married one of her ladies in waiting, Elizabeth Throckmorton, and was scandalised when rumours flew that the baby born to Elizabeth on March 29th the same year was actually the product of her secret marriage to Sir Walter.

Furious that Sir Walter had married without her permission, she threw the pair into the Tower of London in disgrace, and there the two languished (apart from a short spell in September when Sir Walter was released to go and deal with some rioting in Dartmouth) until they found favour with the Queen again and were properly released in December 1592.

Sir Walter and his wife retired to Dorset where at first they tried to modernise the now 400 year old castle. However, the cost of such a venture soon proved too far out of their means, so they settled for building instead a new residence within the nearby deer park. Sir Walter however never lost his love for the picturesque old castle, and continued to spend as much time there as he could.

After Queen Elizabeth I was succeeded by James I, Sir Walter again found himself falling foul of the Crown's will, and spent the last 13 years of his life again imprisoned within the Tower at London, far away from the peace and happiness he had found at his beloved Sherborne. He was beheaded on 29th October 1618.

It is said that every St Michael's Eve Sir Walter returns to walk and sit for a while back in the place he used to love so much – and to smoke a pipe of the tobacco he so famously brought back from his adventures.

St Michael's Eve, or Michaelmas, is a holy day dedicated to St Michael but often marking the changing of the season to autumn. In many areas in Britain a special bread was made to mark the occasion and honour those who were absent or who had died – and it is perhaps this association of turning seasons and times with loved ones lost that brings Sir Walter back to his favourite home on that day.

September 30th

Mytton and Mermaid Hotel, Atcham, Shropshire

The Mytton and mermaid hotel is partially named after John Mytton – more fondly remembered as Mad Jack.
John Mytton was born into a very wealthy family on 30th September 1796, and inherited all that wealth at the tender age of two years old.

He dedicated his life to living howsoever he pleased: and his madcap escapades were truly legendary. To give just a flavour, he kept over 2000 hunting dogs because he liked to hunt so much, and would often strip off to hunt naked on his favourite horse, Baronet.

Baronet was also allowed free roam inside John's ancestral home Halston Hall, much to the chagrin and horror of his servants and peers.

In just 38 short years of life, Mad Jack gambled away or spent his entire inheritance and all of his estates and lands – and finally died in a debtor's prison in Southwark in March 1834.

The only link the hotel claims with him is that his funeral cortege stopped there for a respite on its way to his burial.

Since then, it is said that on the anniversary of his birthday every year Mad Jack returns and haunts the hotel. The story seems inherently unlikely as a reason for a haunting: and indeed I have not been able to find any recent sightings of the ghost.

Chapter 10 - October

October 1st

Audlem Road, Audlem, Cheshire

Barry Cooke wrote in the Warrington Guardian newspaper in 2002 asking for anyone to help him identify the ghost he had now seen twice.

In 2001, on October 1st, a friend and he were driving down the Audlem Road towards Corbrook court at around 12.30am. They suddenly spotted a strange looking man standing out in the road, and as they passed in their car, he stooped downwards as if to peer in through the car windows at them.

As the car passed he disappeared, and even though they later went to check – they could not see any rational explanation for the way he had disappeared from sight so quickly.
They believed from that day that they had seen a ghost.

However, things took an even weirder turn when a year later Barry happened to be driving down the same road.... and saw the same man, who once again disappeared as he passed.

Barry wrote into the papers asking if anyone had experienced the same thing along there or could shed any light on who the apparition might be – but sadly there doesn't seem to be any public record of any replies.

October 9th

Walton Hall Hotel, Stratford Upon Avon, Warwickshire.

The current building, which is a hotel, was built in 1858 by Sir Charles Mordaunt, but there has been a manor on the same site at least as far back as the reign of Queen Elisabeth I. The tale is that once every five years, a pale coloured (some reports say albino) horse gallops riderless through the gardens of the hotel during the night.

Unfortunately, no-one seems to know which year this might fall in, nor why the horse rides. It is quite possible that there is a link to the ghost of a pale young man who is seen within the house itself. One theory about the nature of hauntings says that ghosts slowly fade away with time – becoming paler and then more transplant until only sound is left. Thus it might be that this pale man and pale horse are actually fading remnants of a much older haunting.

There is also supposed to be the ghost of a young child around the stairwell of the house, and when the television series Most Haunted visited in 2016 they claim to have captured the sound of a young child crying out when Yvette Fielding, the host of the show, was recording a speaking piece to camera.

October 11th

Whiddon Park House, near Chagford, Devon
Whiddon Park House was the family seat of the Whiddon family, and was probably first built in the early 1500s. It stands about a mile away from the small town of Chagford, and is surrounded by what was once a magnificent deer park with a high stone wall: symbolising great wealth and status.

The house that currently stands is managed by the National Trust and was built in 1649, some eight years after our ghost tale began.

Mary Whiddon allegedly had two suitors, one of whom became insanely jealous when she chose the other. On her wedding day at the small church at nearby Chagford, the spurned lover made his appearance and shot the bride dead.

Some versions say she was at the altar (and possibly therefore not yet wed) and others claim she was shot as she was leaving the church – having thus enjoyed only a few brief minutes of married life.

Since then, her ghost is said to haunt the building on the anniversary of her death.

Curiously, the only report of her ghost I could actually find, though, was from the Three Crowns Pub in Chagford itself. Some legends claim that there is a secret underground passageway between Whiddon House and the Three Crowns, but don't elucidate as to why this might be the case.

In 1971 there was a wedding party staying at the Three Crowns, and one of the guests awoke to find a spectral bride in a black gown standing in the doorway to his bedroom. As he startled awake and stared at her, she promptly disappeared.

It has allegedly become something of a tradition for brides in Chagford to lay flowers at the tomb of Mary Whiddon to ensure good fortune for their own marriages.

Historically, very little is known of Mary, since records of the area from the Civil War period have all long since been lost.

All we can say for sure is that there was a Mary Whiddon who died on 11th October 1641, and her tomb is in the church there. On it a small poem is inscribed, which claims that Mary died "a matron, yet a maid". This could be interpreted as "married, but still a virgin", which would of course be the case if she were shot on her wedding day, but could also mean "married, but still very young".

The inscription does not say how she died, nor does it mention a wedding day or a husband. The only written record left of Mary is her will, and it is written in the name of Mary Whiddon, which means she was either still unmarried when she wrote the will and subsequently died, or married a cousin with the same surname, since her tomb clearly says she was married (the term matron meant a married woman). The inscription on her tomb mentions nothing tragic about her death at all – but the wording would have been chosen by a grieving family whatever the cause of death and they may well not have wished to point out the horror.

October 12th

Hampton Court Palace, Molesey, London

The story of Jane Seymour, the third wife of King Henry VIII, is actually a terribly sad one. Jane had been a lady in waiting to both of the King's previous wives, and historians remain divided to this day as to whether she or her family were cleverly scheming to get her into a position of power, or whether she was just where the Kings roving eye fell next as Anne Boleyn fell out of favour.

Whatever the truth, Jane and the King were betrothed to marry within 24 hours of Anne Boleyn losing her head on the block, with the King still desperate after 28 years on the throne to produce for himself a male heir.

The King and Jane were married in May 1536, and on 12th October 1537, Jane gave birth to the long awaited Royal Prince, who was named Edward.

The King was beside himself with joy, but the happiness was short lived as Jane succumbed to complications following the birth – probably a fever – and died just 12 days later.

Whatever the truth behind whether she was a politically savvy woman scheming to get power or just a young girl who happened to catch the King's eye, no mother should have to leave her child so soon and never get the chance to see them grow up.

It is hardly surprising then that it is said that every October 12th, marking the birth of her beloved boy, her ghost can be seen carrying a candle and ascending the staircase to the area where the royal apartments she occupied used to be.

Curiously, in 2015 a coach driver visiting the Palace with his coachload of sightseers captured the image of a young woman peering down through the main entrance staircase and has speculated that this might be the image of one of king Henry VIII's wives. You can see the image in the Mirror newspaper for 28.12.2015.

October 13th

Charfield, Gloucestershire

In the early morning hours of Saturday 13th October 1928, a mail/passenger train passing through Charfield hit a goods train. The collision derailed the passenger train, which then hit another goods train coming the other way. At that time, trains were still illuminated using gaslights.

In the crash, the gas cannisters from the lighting in the passenger train were broken, and the escaping gas became trapped below the bridge. It soon ignited and the first seven carriages caught fire – spreading an inferno through the wreckage and in total claiming the lives of 16 people.

The weather was described variously as heavy mist or very foggy that morning, and it seems that the drivers of the passenger train did not see the warning light which should have told them to slow down and stop as there was a hazard on the line.

Tragic as it was, the matter would have rested there, but as the clean-up operation began, a real mystery began to unfold.

The passengers killed in the fire were so badly charred by the time the fire was extinguished, that one body could not be reliably distinguished from another. They were identified in general by their belongings and by their relatives coming forward saying they had been in the train. Rather than have the possibility of the wrong relative buried in the wrong grave due to the difficulty in accurate identification, it was agreed that there would be a mass grave for all of the bodies.

However, time started to pass and two of the bodies remained unidentified and unclaimed. They were thought to be the bodies of two children – aged perhaps 7 years old and 12 years old or thereabouts. The Doctor who attended the victims and gave the death certificates was certain that he had identified the bodies of two children amongst the remains, and the police who helped clear the train corroborated his findings.

Furthermore, a porter who had been on the train earlier confirmed that he had seen two children sitting in the forward carriage together, but knew nothing further about them nor noticed who they were with – if indeed they were with anyone.

Some members of the public began to doubt there ever were two children on the train, as it seemed inconceivable that they were travelling alone on the overnight train at such a tender age, and even more inexplicable that no-one came forward to claim them in death.

However, the doctor, the police and the porter remained adamant that there had been two children and that they had died in the crash, right up until their own deaths years later.

The mystery deepened when the villagers at Charfield noticed that every October 13th a chauffeur driven limousine would pull up at the churchyard where the mass grave and memorial plaque were sited, and a woman dressed in black and hidden by a mourning veil would lay a small posy of flowers at the grave before leaving again. It seems she never spoke to anyone and no-one knows who she was. Her visits continued right up until the early 1960s.

Some witnesses have claimed over the years that they still sometimes see her black form in the graveyard – and also that two children can sometimes be seen standing hand in hand on the rail tracks, staring forlornly into the distance as if waiting for someone to come and collect them.

Local ghost hunters Joshua and Michael Hall visited the site on the anniversary in 2017, but were unable to find any trace of either the woman or the children.

October 14th

Battle Abbey, Battle, East Sussex

The Battle of Hastings was fought on October 14th on a field in East Sussex, and raged for over nine hours, from dawn to dusk, as both sides fought desperately for the future of England.

William of Normandy was ultimately victorious, famously winning when King Harold of the English was killed by an arrow through his eye. The Norman Conquest was set and the fate of England sealed.

In 1070, William the Conqueror, as the new King became known, commissioned an Abbey to be built on the site of the battle, the ruins of which can still be visited today as a National Heritage site.

Today, the ruins themselves are haunted by various ghosts of monks and ladies which can be seen at any time of the year – there are numerous reports to be found. For example, in 2001 a photo was taken which seems to show a spectral figure hanging in one of the doorways, and in 2002, a school teacher visiting the abbey asked about the member of staff she had just seen dressed in period costume as a monk. There was no-one in costume on site that day.

In September 2006 the Ghost Club conducted an overnight investigation, and their full report can be read on their web site.

They documented the fact that in one particular location a lot of their equipment suddenly suffered from battery drain, and an inexplicable tremble underfoot was felt.

Shortly after the batteries in all of their electrical equipment drained, footsteps were heard and in another area a shadow figure was seen. One theory is that batteries are drained by spirits looking to find an energy source to help them materialize.

The anniversary of the battle each year is said to produce the sounds of men fighting, and sometimes the sight of a knight riding across the field. Despite all the various reports of the general year-round hauntings, I could not find any date specific records.

October 16th

Conington, Cambridgeshire

The landscape around Conington, a little way south of Peterborough, is flat fenland, which can sometimes generate an eerie feeling all of its own.

In 1948, a truck carrying some German prisoners of war was hit by a train on the railway crossing close to the village, killing six men.

Later the same year a soldier called Colonel Mellows opened the gates (which were manually operated at that time) and started to ease his black Chrysler car across, watched by his friend who was travelling with him and who intended to close the gates behind them.

The friend later described how they were both side-tracked by looking over at the station buildings, and neither of them noticed the 4.00pm London train bearing inexorably down on them from the other direction until it was too late – and both the Colonel and his black Labrador dog who was in the car with him were killed instantly.

One source I found says the truck with the Germans in it was struck by lightning, rather than a train.

It is said that once a manned signal box was installed, the signal box men would often hear the Colonel's ghost by the gates or the sound of his car when none was there – although some thought it might actually be one of the German soldiers they could hear.

My husband and I visited the site in a high wind on the anniversary in 2017, but the sheer number of trains now passing through – literally every three or four minutes – meant that hearing anything or sensing anything above the noise of the trains, the waiting cars, the tractor working in the neighbouring field, and the sound of the machinery operating the crossing itself was impossible.

Undeterred even by the remnants of Hurricane Ophelia blowing Sahara dust high in the atmosphere and causing a strangely eerie orange glow in the sky, I took a number of pictures in the hope of capturing something the eye could not discern, but to no avail.

October 20th

Eastgate Street, Bury St Edmunds, Suffolk

In 1935, two young girls were walking home with their mother along Eastgate Street in Bury St Edmunds. Eastgate Street runs along the side if the famous Abbey Gardens, and at that time there was a small unbuilt in area of rough vegetation alongside the street which was known as The Glen.

As the family walked along, a sudden gust of wind sprang out of nowhere, and in its wake they could suddenly see what appeared to be a wounded man in his underwear being helped across the road by a young female nurse dressed in a very old fashioned uniform. She helped her charge into The Glen and out of sight of the astonished trio of onlookers.

Moments later, to their horror, a gunshot rang out followed by a lady's scream. The mother gathered her two daughters and hastily beat a retreat to safety and to seek help.

It turned out they were witnessing the re-enactment of the murder of a wounded soldier from the time of the Crimean War. He was on leave being nursed by Mary Treese, who, much to the chagrin of her father, fell in love with her handsome charge. The father had pursued the fleeing pair and shot Mary's lover in front of her – and every 20th October the tragic scene replays itself.

Apparently, the father was then hanged for his crime – so Mary suffered a double tragedy.

I could not find any records of any other sightings, so it is difficult to see why this has earned the title of being an anniversary ghost if it was only ever seen once. It seems more likely to me that it might have been a time slip type of haunting – if in fact there was any truth to the original story at all.

October 21st

Betty Potters Dip, Boxted, Essex

Running into the small village of Boxted, in Essex, is Boxted Straight Road. Very aptly named, it is a perfectly straight bit of road, except for the slight bend with a dip, which has become known locally as Betty Potter's Dip. In 1815 it was recorded that the rent from Betty Potter's Piece ("piece" being an old name for a small field) was being used to fund a charity to aid the poor of the parish.

The story goes that in the 1640s a local woman named Betty Potter had her cottage here, and she was widely believed to be a witch. She had offered cures for ailments and the like which people were happy to avail themselves of, but the villagers also spread the rumour that she had bewitched the horses who were pulling a wagon of wheat, causing them to spill their valuable load.

This was the dark time in our history when Matthew Hopkins, the Witchfinder General, was active, and hysteria was rife about the perils of harbouring witches amongst godly folk. In response to the rumours, the squire's son and a gang of local men dragged poor Betty from her cottage on the night of 21st October and hanged her from a nearby tree.

Another version of the story says that Elizabeth Potter was a local lady who committed suicide by hanging herself from a tree in the 1700s.

Either way, since then, the hapless woman's ghost is said to haunt the tree and the road at the time of her death. I have not found any accounts of anyone who has ever actually seen her.

October 22nd

Poynton Green, Shropshire

There is a strange little legend associated with this tiny hamlet in Shropshire. The story goes that two World War II Czechoslovakian pilots were killed here when their plane crashed in the field on 22 October 1941.

The local farmer ran out into the field to try and save the pilots, but was beaten back by the intense heat of the flames, and both pilots died. He claimed however to have seen a cat emerge from the wreckage, and seek shelter with a neighbouring old lady. The cat vanished when the old lady eventually died, and no-one knew what became of it, but once every ten years, it can again be seen at the site of the crash.

The difficulty with the story is that I can't find any record of a plane crash here. There **was** an aircraft shot down that day in Shropshire, but it was 22 miles away in Woore, near Market Drayton. It had four crew – two of whom bailed out and were taken prisoner, the other two remained in the burning craft as it plummeted to the ground and were killed in the resulting impact.

October 23rd

Edgehill Battle site, Warwickshire

On this date in 1642, the first pitched battle of the English Civil War took place at Edgehill. Over 30,000 men took part in the battle, which raged on for some hours and took hundreds of lives on both sides. The battle was not particularly decisive in its outcome, and some sources have claimed that the dead were left where they fell for some three months after the fracas.

The claim is, that not long before Christmas that same year, some shepherds crossing the fields late at night saw to their horror the battle being re-enacted in the sky above them – complete with full sound and colour – with such detail that individual soldiers could be identified.

They called in a clergyman and a judge to witness the horror, and people from roundabout gathered night after night to watch the terrible spectacle. Eventually the King himself heard the tale, and sent out a Royal Commission to investigate. It is alleged that they too witnessed the phenomena, and reported their eerie findings back to the King. The local villagers then buried the decomposing corpses to try and put an end to the ghostly shenanigans, and the activity died down.

We actually get this information from a pamphlet which was published a few months after the event. In those days, pamphlets were the forerunners of newspapers, but very often gave spectacular accounts of events in order to pass across some particular moral message. In this case, it was aimed at giving the subtle message that for a country to go against its King was against the natural order of things and would cause terrible retribution and heavenly disapproval in the form of supernatural horrors plaguing the countryside.

However, the reporting of ghostly battle sounds and in particular the sight of a galloping horse in the area where the battle took place have persisted over the years. One Youtube video displays the voice recordings of some interviews on the subject done in the 1950s of some supposed eye witness.

One man tells how in 1915 he was coming home on a cart with a sturdy mare, and jumped down to open the gate whilst his companion steered the cart through. However, as he stood there, a grey horse galloped through, and so disturbed the mare that she bolted. On finally catching her and reaching the next village they were told they had witnessed the ghost horse and that was why their sturdy old mare spooked so badly.

Another interview is with a well-to-do sounding lady, who describes recently driving her car across the area, only to suddenly feel very strongly that she was driving through a throng of people, all jostling around the car shoulder to shoulder. For a brief moment she actually caught sight of the face of one man, which she describes in quite detail.

Having spent years during my career as an interviewer myself, however, I am very sceptical about the tapes. People simply don't talk that lucidly when recalling an event – they criss-cross their own time line and their recollections meander as a thought pops into their head: it is the interviewer who normally sorts the information gleaned into a semblance of order, and then checks it over with the interviewee for accuracy. In these recordings, although one speaks with a posh accent and the other with a "rural peasant" accent – both speak in the flow of a story: sounding like they are practised actors reading from a script.

I did find an account from a nearby RAF station which said that their dogs would refuse to go out on night patrol on the anniversary of the battle, and I would be very curious to hear from any ghost investigation teams as to whether they have ever found any activity there.

October 29th

The Mermaid Inn, Rye, Sussex

The Mermaid Inn is a stunningly picturesque half-timbered structure, facing onto the charmingly cobbled Mermaid Lane. Its cellars, belonging to an earlier building on the site, date back as far as 1156 a.d., whilst the rest of the current building dates to 1420, after an incursion by the French burnt the original hostelry down.

It was once used by a smuggling gang known as the Hawkhurst gang – who were particular brutal to anyone who crossed them. There is one tale about the gang which claims that they dealt with one customs officer who was trying to apprehend them by burying the poor man alive.

There are numerous hauntings all year round within the building, so it is probably always worth a visit, but the one which interests us supposedly happens on 23rd October every year.

Surprisingly then, there only seems to have been one sighting of it – which in itself suggests urban legend rather than fact.

Supposedly on that night, a pair of men fighting with swords can be seen or sometimes heard, and the victor pushes the corpse of the other into a stairwell. No-one seems to be offering an explanation of who they were or why they fight on that date.

You can see investigation videos from 2007 and 2009 on Youtube, and the T.V. programme "Most Haunted" also visited it – as did others.

I'll leave it to you to look at the videos online and decide whether the tale is urban myth, or a case of "no smoke without fire".

October 30th

Lydiard Millicent Manor House, Lydiard Millicent, Wiltshire

Tracing this ghost story has proved more than a little difficult – and truly fascinating from the point of view of how myths grow! Lydiard Millicent and Lydiard Tregoze are two adjoining villages in Wiltshire. Between them lies the magnificent park of Lydiard House, which is currently owned and managed by Swindon Borough Council as a conference centre, museum, and country park.

Almost everywhere you try to read about the October ghost, you will see an account, very sparse in detail, that each anniversary of her fiancé's murder, the ghost of what is thought to be Lady Blunt appears in the garden – or her screams can be heard echoing in the night. One account says she has been doing this for the 200 years since her death – which would put her sometime in the late 1700s or early 1800s.

The trouble is that Lydiard House was owned by the St John family (pronounced Sin Jin) for around 400 years until it was sold in the first half of the 20th Century.

I can't find any tale of a Lady Blunt there – or anything about her poor fiancé.

However, I became intrigued when some accounts would refer to Lydiard House at Lydiard Tregoze, others to Lydiard House at Lydiard Millicent – and some to just the Manor House at Lydiard Millicent. Are all the accounts referring to the same place? After all, the magnificent pallandine design Lydiard House and its park lies between the two villages, so I guess you could refer to it either way depending on how you were looking at it or which direction you were travelling to it from.

But interestingly – there *was* a Manor House and its holdings at Lydiard Millicent which was a significant property as far back as 900 a.d. This Manor and the land it possessed went through numerous guises and owners as the centuries passed. It had already begun to decline in size and status by the late 1560's, but then many of its holdings (farmsteads and woodlands) were sold off piecemeal to different families.

By 1739 the much reduced Lydiard Millicent Manor was left by Sir John Askew to his brother Ferdinando – who in turn left it to his daughter Mary, the wife of Henry Blunt.

On her death, Mary Blunt passed the house on down through the Blunt line.

Eventually, the Lydiard Millicent Manor (now known as Manor Farm) burned down in 1880, but in the 1960s a new house was built on the site using much of the old stone and was called Manor House.

I rather suspect that it is *here* that the mysterious "Lady Blunt" who grieves the death of her fiancé haunts, and not nearby at the magnificent Lydiard Park – and that's why there aren't any actual sightings of her recorded there that I can find! Sadly though, it seems the actual detail of the tale is long since lost.

October 31st

October 31st is today best known for being Halloween, when children dress up and go trick or treating and people carve faces into pumpkins and light candles within.

It has long been a festival day – originally (and still for many) as Samhain, the Celtic feast for the end of harvest and the beginning of winter.

It was also one of the "seminal" days of the year: so called as this is when the veil separating this word from the next was at its thinnest, and the dead could briefly return to their homes. Historically, at the feast tables, an extra place was set at table for precisely the purpose of allowing the dead to join the living.

The feast day, like so many others from Celtic tradition, was subsumed into the Christian festival of All Hallows on 1st November – hence the night before becoming All Hallows Eve and gradually shortened to Halloween.

It's hardly surprising then that so many anniversary type hauntings fall on this day: when the dead are traditionally said to be welcome to visit with the living. Many of the following stories seem to have little to do with the actual date: which tends to confirm the suspicion that they are merely linked to this date because that is the night when all ghosts traditionally walk the same plane as us.

Cliviger Gorge, Burnley, Lancashire

Cliviger Gorge lies roughly between the towns of Burnley in Lancashire and Todmorden in West Yorkshire.
It holds a wonderful old legend – which has clearly morphed and changed over the years.

There are various versions you can find to read – the most common of which seems to be the tale of Sir William Townseley and his lady love, Lady Sybil. She was intent on practising the dark arts, and sold her soul to the Devil in exchange for powers.

However Sir William employed the aid of a local witch, Mother Helston, and together they captured the milk white doe which Lady Sybil had changed herself into.

Mother Helston turned herself into a hunting hound who chased and eventually captured the doe, then Sir William placed a noose around its neck and led it back to his home, where after certain spells and incantations the Lady Sybil was released from the Devil's grasp and Sir William and Lady Sybil were able to marry and live happily ever after.

Other versions mention a man who murdered his lover and buried her here, whilst others say Lady Sybil is buried here, and others say the hunter in question was not Sir William but a man called Gabriel Ratchetts.

In actual fact, the name Gabriel Ratchetts or Gabble Ratchetts is given to the Lancashire version of the Black Shuck – or hellhounds. Some say they were part of the Wild Hunt, and would fly the night skies looking for souls of the dead or the living to steal away.

The oldest tales however seem only to speak of a demonic entity – or a "frightful hirsute demon" who lived in the Gorge.

Since hirsute means covered in hair – one can't help but think about the mutation of myths over the years, and the modern day sightings of Sasquatch or Bigfoot elsewhere in the world.

In fact one author, Thomas Booth, wrote in 1883 not of the legend of the wild hunt or black dogs, but rather of the Towneley Boggart – an evil sprite who haunted the area in retribution for the fact that the Towneley family had been responsible for enclosing the land around here and claiming ownership under the Enclosure Acts from 1604 onwards. The Gentleman's magazine mentioned the sprite as far back as 1821.

Some say that the sprites, or boggarts, have declined in number because of the encroachment of civilisation and the enclosure of the wild lands into domestic fields – so is it possible that for a time some wild cryptozoological creature did linger in the protection the Cliviger Gorge offered?

It might be as well to be especially vigilant if you choose to go hiking there! Take a camera if you go... you might get the first ever picture of a boggart.

Armboth Hall, Lake District

Armboth Fell is a domed plateau sitting roughly in the centre of the Lake District, in Allerdale. Before the area was flooded, as it is now, to form Thirlmere Reservoir, it used to be a steeply sided valley with two distinct areas of water, thinning in the middle where they were spanned by an ancient bridge called the Celtic Bridge. On one side of this there used to sit a building called Armboth Hall. In 1847 it was advertising as a guest house for tourists

Armboth Hall, or House, or Farm (depending on which source you read) is actually now below the waters of the reservoir, but there is still a monkey puzzle tree standing, which used to be in its grounds. As far back as 1855 it was being listed as a haunted property: when it had a reputation for lights being seen at night which should not have been there.

The tale went that the house would sometimes seem as if it were being prepared for a wedding, with lights and sounds of crockery and so on and a peal of bells, then a black dog would be seen swimming across the lake. It was also said that when viewed from 2 or 3 miles distant at night, its lights would shine on the water in such a way as to make it appear a grand mansion, instead of the more humble house it actually was.

The back story behind the haunting is said to be that the daughter of the house was due to be married on November 1st. The night before the nuptials were due to take place, the servants were in the middle of readying the hall for the official wedding banquet, when the lady's body was found drowned in the lake below the house. At the time, some suspected that the culprit was in fact her fiancé.

The year of this happening, or the lady's identity, seems unfortunately to be unknown. The house was owned from around the late 1590s to the late 1890s by the Jackson family, and the legend doesn't seem to relate to any of their daughters – so one must presume it predates them. Whatever the truth, the house was felt to be unlucky ever after that, and it was felt to draw to it the ghosts of any souls who had died wrongfully.

The swimming dog mentioned in the tale is probably a reference to the Cumbrian Cappel – another "Black Shuck" type manifestation and known to be a harbinger of death. The whole valley was also said to be haunted by "boggles", another name for the "boggart" or demonic entity.

There is a video taken around Thirlmere which you can watch on YouTube – it was taken in 2013 and is titled Haunted Lake, Thirlmere. It claims to capture spirit faces in the water and spirit orbs. Watch it for yourself and decide what you think – personally I am certain one of the orbs is just a froth of bubbles from the waterfall and the rest is just pareidolia (the human mind seeing facial images in patterns as mentioned earlier).

Minsden Chapel, Chapelfoot, Hertfordshire

Minsden chapel is today a weathered ruin only accessible on foot, and is located a little to the south of Hitchin. It was built in the 1500s and fell into disrepair a couple of hundred years later, finally falling out of use completely in the 1800s.

If you do get a chance to visit the site at midnight on October 31st, it is said that you could encounter the ghost of a monk climbing the stairs that have long since disappeared. At other times, the bells (which were lost in the 1700s) can still be heard ringing, and sometimes the ghost of a small child can be seen there.

There was a famous photo of the ghost taken in 1907, but the photographer finally admitted some thirty years later that he had faked it using the technique of double exposure.

Peter Underwood, the great ghost investigator also once spent a night there, and heard the sound of distant music.

Photographs of the chapel usually show the iconic archway, but unfortunately even this finally succumbed to the ravages of time and disintegrated in 2008.

There have been some rumours in 2017 that it will be sold to a private landowner, and will then no longer be open to the public.

In 2010 one ghost hunting outfit published a series of short videos of their investigation there which are easily found under "Almost Haunted - Minsden Chapel". They thought they heard voices and footsteps at one point.

Other teams visited in 2011, 2014 and 2016, and posted their video results: they are easily found if you want to see and listen to what they heard and sensed. Clearly the site still attracts a lot of interest and is still thought to be very active.

One couple of lady investigators heard the sound of heavy boots walking up to them, the sound of voices, and the sound of bells ringing but unfortunately didn't capture any of it on video.

It's a bit of a walk up to the chapel – so if you are wanting to visit and if it is still open to the public – go prepared for a muddy hike and wear suitable clothing.

Netley Abbey, Netley, Hampshire

Managed today by English Heritage, Netley Abbey is a beautiful ruin with free entry to the public during the summer months. It stands close to the coast just south-east of Southampton.

It was founded in 1238 a.d. for the Cistercian monks, and probably housed around 45 people. It fell out of favour in 1536 with Henry VIII's dissolution of the monasteries, and was granted to Sir William Paulet in recognition of his services to the King. He converted the buildings into a stylish Tudor mansion house with a grand courtyard. Unfortunately little of his additions remain today as they were mostly in brick, and were removed a couple of hundred years later when it again fell into disrepair. By the 1840s, people were visiting it for picnics and such and basking in its picturesque setting of overgrown ruins. Still later, the encroaching undergrowth was removed to give proper sight of the remaining stonework.

I have been unable to determine why the ghost of the monk so often reported here is linked to Halloween, since the modern day sightings seem to be from all times of year, day or night!

In the 1950's one lady walking her dog one evening saw a dark figure walk across the grass of the abbey and then suddenly disappear. During the whole incident, her dog was whining piteously and trying to run away from the area. Needless to say, she never walked near the abbey at night again.

In July 1985 a husband and wife ghost hunting team saw a dark shadow pass across the ruins in front of them – as if a man had walked by when in fact there was no one else present.

In 2004 a paranormal investigation team felt they had seen the figure of a man dressed in a pale robe, and later on another figure dressed in a dark robe. They heard chanting at one point for which they could find no natural explanation.

In 2005 photographer Andrew Nicholson took a snap in broad daylight of the abbey when visiting with family. One of the shots shows what looks like a hooded figure standing beneath one of the archways. Andrew is absolutely certain no-one living was there when he took the photo.

Town Hall, Bournemouth, Dorset

Bournemouth Townhall was built in the late 1880s and was originally the Mont Dore Hotel. During World War I it was used as a military hospital and then a convalescent home for British and Indian soldiers returning from the front.

The story is that every October 31st a soldier dressed in uniform from that period helps himself to a drink of water from the public water fountain. Some sources tell the story but do not link the occurrence to any specific date.

In February 2004 UK Ghost Investigations conducted an investigation inside the building and you can read their report on line – they picked up some noises of squeaking wheels, some doors creaking as if trying to open, and sensed a very oppressive atmosphere in the small hours of the morning which they had not sensed earlier in the night.

In July 2011 the Dorset Ghost Hunters visited the site and investigated from outside the building. They picked up what they believe is the image of a soldier on their video camera. They also felt that they had some success with the "spirit box" – a device which scans backwards and forwards rapidly across radio frequencies, never stopping on any particular radio signal. The idea is that spirits can manipulate it to pick out words in response to questions. You can listen to their session on line and see what you think.

There does not seem to be any account of why the soldier haunts or what is significant about the date.

Bonnewells Lane, Bransby, Lincolnshire

This is an odd entry to be including – but here goes! Bransby is a small hamlet to the north west of Lincoln. The only reference I found to this apparent ghost was from the Paranormal Database, which mentioned that on Halloween each year, Bonnewells Lane in Bransby was haunted by a spectral sow and her piglets running along the lane.

Unfortunately – I can't find any such lane in Bransby (or anywhere in fact) and neither can I find anyone giving details of the mystery pig!

I'm including this story in the hope someone somewhere will know more and will write in to enlighten me.

Hawkesdale Hall, Dalston, Cumbria

Originally there was a building called Hawkesdale Low Hall here, about which very little is known. It was replaced in the late 1600s by Hawkesdale Hall. The building went up for sale in 2012, and I presume it is still privately owned.

There is a legend that on Halloween each year, the ghost of a young man who hanged himself in the hall can be seen leaving the hall carrying a candle. He glides down to the nearby River Caldew, where he vanishes into the cold waters. I cannot find any further detail about this haunting, and to me it sounds much more like a traditional corpse candle type story – again linked purely to the night that the souls of the dead can return to the earthly plane once more.

Hindlip Hall, Hindlip, Worcestershire

The original building was built before 1575, and has had a colourful history with its links to the Gunpowder Plot and Guy Fawkes. Today, it is the headquarters of the West Mercia Police. It's tempting to speculate whether any spooks dare make an appearance with so many policemen around.

When the Gunpowder plot was discovered and foiled, everyone connected to it fled as best they could. Two priests, Father Oldcorne and Father Garnett, fled as far as Hindlip Hall, along with Nicholas Owen and his apprentice and they were secreted away into priest holes by their friends there.

They survived there for a number of days in January 1606 before eventually they were discovered and seized when they began to starve. Owen was tortured and died "when his bowels burst" on the rack – the others were hung, drawn and quartered.

Since then, it is said that every Halloween the Lady of the house, Mary Habington, continues to make her ghostly rounds to the priest holes as she did in life – when she brought scraps of sustenance and water to the holy men hiding within her walls. Quite why she should do this in October when the events took place in January is again probably linked to the belief that this date was one when the dead could return in ghostly form.

In 1974 the remains of a secret tunnel were discovered running from the cellars out into the gardens and it is believed this was originally meant to be an escape route from the priest holes within the house.

St Lawrence Church and Rectory, Abbots Langley, Hertfordshire

A much more recent ghost haunts the two properties and the roadway between them.

Mary-Ann Treble was the housekeeper for the rectory.

According to the renowned author and ghost hunter Peter Underwood, she was led a terrible life by the Vicar's wife, who was cruel to her housekeeper and never let her have sufficient warmth in her room or food to eat. Eventually Mary-Ann died of her ill treatment – and ever since then her ghost is likely to pull the fireplace off the wall in revenge for never being allowed to properly use it.

Other versions of the story say that she died when she fell down the stairs at the Rectory – and again, some say the mistress of the house pushed her, and others that it was a simple accident.

Her ghost was said to be very active in the first half of the century until eventually Bishop Furse was called to lay her spirit and there seems to have been little mention of her since then.

Lesnes Abbey, London Borough of Bexley

Lesnes Abbey was founded in 1178 by one of the men involved in the murder of Thomas a Becket as an act of penance. It survived until the Dissolution of the Monasteries in 1536, when most of it was torn down. Over the following centuries a lot of the stone was robbed and recycled into other buildings.

Today the site has been restored for visitors to be able to trace the layout of the original abbey and see what few stone remains are left standing, and is owned and managed by the London Borough of Bexley. One of its main claims to fame is the discovery in an archaeological dig of the remains in an ornate box of the heart of one Roesia, who was the great granddaughter of the founder of the abbey, and who spent much of her young life there. So fond was she of her childhood home that when she died she requested her heart be taken back to the place she had loved so dearly and buried there.

Sitting as it does so close to the heart of London, just south of the River Thames, it is surprising to find the abbey ruins still boast an extensive area of surrounding woodland, and many people say that the woods, even though they are now a nature reserve, are far more eerie than the abbey ruins themselves.

The story is that on Halloween each year, the ghost of a monk who was killed because he broke his vows of chastity returns to haunt his former home.

Interestingly, in July 2016 a home owner who uses CCTV to monitor the security of the front of his modern day urban residential property in a street close to the abbey ruins caught what seems to be a partial, transparent human figure walking about in the road outside his house.

Rossall School, Fleetwood, Lancashire

Rossall School was founded in 1844 and continues to run today as a private day pupil and boarding school. It sits in a truly stunning location right on the shore's edge just above the popular seaside resort of Blackpool.

Every Halloween, the ghost of a lady in white crosses the school grounds – and although originally it is said she would scream as she would go, the aural part of her appearance appears to have died out. She was first written about as far as I can see as long ago as 1894. She seems to have gained the name "Lady Fleetwood" over time, but that is probably more to do with the name of the area than anything else.

Sometimes a black monk is also seen wandering the grounds of the school, and also along the seafront itself. One former pupil commenting on a recent Facebook page recalls seeing him during her time at the school, so it would seem there is still activity there today. The school also seems to occasionally run ghost tours which might be worth a visit if you are in the area around this time of year.

Cliffs at Amble, Northumberland

There is a very scant mention of the ghost of a woman who is seen to fling herself off the cliffs at Amble, not far from Cliff House, every Halloween.

I could not find any sightings of her, nor could I find any explanations as to who she might have been or why she committed suicide.

I did find one blog reply from 2012 where a reader commented that he had lived in Amble his entire life and had never heard this ghost story. Interestingly, he also quoted as the source the only source I had found – which to my mind gives the story very little validity or credibility if only one source has used it.

Whitby, North Yorkshire

When Henry VIII decided to tear down the monasteries and abbeys across his Kingdom in defiance of the Roman Catholic Church, Whitby Abbey was one of those unfortunate institutions which did not escape the Dissolution.
Legend says that to make matters worse, not only did the King order the Abbey torn down, but he had its bells loaded on a ship to be taken to London, where they would be sold.

Unfortunately, no sooner had the ship set sail than a sudden storm sprang out of nowhere, sinking the ship and its cargo still within sight of the Abbey.

Since then, the legend is that the bells can be heard ringing mournfully from beneath the waves every Halloween, when the veil between this world and the next is at its thinnest.
I'm not aware, though, of anyone reporting that they have actually heard them.

Cley Hill

See 15th March for the full entry.

Crebilly Road, Ballymena, County Antrim, Ireland

A rather daring highwayman decided to rob one of the wealthy houses along this road, and tried to make his escape on horseback with his bag of loot. Unfortunately for him, the guards strung a piece of wire across the gateposts, so as he rode through at full gallop in his haste to get away, his head was severed clean from his body.

Since then, his headless ghost, still on horseback, can sometimes be seen or heard roaming this road on Halloween. One or two other versions seem to exist – the most colourful is that the local squire argued with his lover, and tore away from the house on his horse. So angry was he about their quarrel that he did not wait for the gates to be opened but instead tried to force his horse to jump them – but was flung from his mount and decapitated when he hit the spikes on top of the gate.

Legends of headless horsemen abound all over the British isles, and it is quite possible that many of them were created originally to deter people from wandering certain areas at night – when rather than encounter the ghost, they might encounter instead the local gang of smugglers and blow their cover.

Court Oak Pub, Harborne, Birmingham, West Midlands

The Court Oak Pub has a very strange ghost who apparently tends to make his presence known around Halloween every year. According to one story in the Daily Mirror in 2011, regulars have nicknamed him "Corky" because he likes to smash wine bottles down in the cellar when no one is actually present – but only bottles of the cheaper wine!

The building itself only dates back to 1932, but it is claimed that it stands on the site of an old gibbet post – where people would have been hung for various crimes.

In September 2010 one paranormal investigation team recorded their findings following an investigation at the pub on YouTube which you can view. They claim there is a spirit of a girl who was wrongfully accused of murdering her baby and hanged still present there. A word of caution though – the music on the video is intensely irritating.

Chapter 11 – November

Coopers Arms, St Margarets Street, Rochester, Kent

There has been a building on this site since at least 1199 a.d. when a house was built for the monks of the nearby St Andrews priory. With the dissolution of the abbeys under the reign of King Henry VIII, the house fell into disuse and was purchased by a private buyer, who turned it into a hostelry. He opened his doors for business after some renovation work to the building in 1543, and called his establishment The Coopers' Tavern, in memory of the years the monks had lived there. The building is still a pub now, and has on its wall a print giving the names of all the landlords from 1543 until now.

A cooper is someone who makes the barrels and caskets that wine, beer, or spirits were stored in – and the monks and the abbey were well known for the wine and ale they brewed.

Supposedly, one of the monks broke his vow of chastity and got a young lady of the parish pregnant – and for his crime he was walled up alive in the cellars of the house where he and his brethren lived.

Since then, most especially on November nights, his spirit can still be seen walking across the bar and through the wall in the pub. Some versions say that a woman in white clutching a baby can also be seen running down the road outside the pub, and that the monks ghost, having walked through the wall, follows her. One blog writer recalled that in the 1970s, it was quite common to see a pint glass slide slowly towards the edge of the bar, which would have to be caught before it fell. This was always attributed to the ghostly monk.

In actual fact the practice of immurement or "walling up" was less commonplace as a form of death sentence than one might suppose, given how often it seems to appear in folklore.

Much more common was the lesser form of "Vade in Pacem" immurement, where the culprit was, to use modern parlance, sentenced to solitary confinement. This was often a life sentence, and often in very small cramped chambers – but the person was fed and watered. Many died very quickly from the sheer despair and horror this plunged them into.

That being said, Benedictine monks (as were the ones at St Andrew's Priory), did have vows of chastity, and when the Bishop visited in 1439 he was annoyed enough by the state of affairs there that he issued injunctions that the monks were to start obeying the rules properly. So perhaps our poor monk did indeed suffer some such fate before remaining forever after as a spirit.

Vinegar Hill, Marham, Norfolk

In 1249 a.d. the Abbey at Marham was founded and was dedicated to the Virgin Mary, St Barbara and St Edmund. It usually housed up to 15 nuns. Today, all that is left of it is a few ruined walls, listed as an ancient monument, and sited on private land.

The legend goes that one nun, Sister Barbara, devised a plan to increase the wealth of her Abbey. She would pay a band of robbers to wait on the dark, high sided narrow lane which crossed nearby Vinegar Hill, and which was actually then the main route between Swaffham and Kings Lynn.

The robbers would waylay wealthy travellers, knocking them unconscious and stealing their goods and finery. They would then carry their unconscious victim to the Abbey, where Sister Barbara would pay them for her cut of the deal.

She and her fellow nuns would then nurse the hapless traveller back to consciousness and health, and would have them believe that they themselves had "rescued" the hapless traveller from their probable death at the hands of the brigands. The victims and their grateful families then often bestowed valuable gifts on the "pious and saintly" nuns.

Eventually the monks at the nearby Pentney Abbey grew suspicious of how the nuns were living with such apparent wealth, and kept watch on Sister Barbara until they had proof – whereupon she was convicted of her greedy crimes and as punishment bricked up alive in the walls.

Since then, it is said, her forlorn ghosts can be seen gliding along Vinegar Hill on November nights, revisiting the scene of her fall from grace.

In truth, the very last Abbess of the Abbey was in fact called Barbara Mason, and she was incumbent from 1511 to 1535. It was she who was at the helm when King Henry VIII decided to follow his course of the dissolution of the abbeys and monasteries around England, which at that time were holding a lot of the land and therefore power around the country.

Often, it seems that scandals were created by the officers of the King in order to gain popular support and justify the actions of destroying the religious communities – but it is always possible that there was some truth in the case of Marham Abbey and Abbess Barbara.

The "Comperta Monastica" of 1536 stated that Abbess Barbara and four of her nuns had confessed to "*grave incontinency*" and a later report said there were "*religious persons of slaunderous reporte*" at the Abbey.

Certainly there was listed a fair bit of wealth in the inventory taken – including a Cope of green Bruges satin. (A cope is the religious outer cloak decorated with symbols etc worn in Catholic religious ceremonies). There is no report of a punishment for the Abbess, but she and her four nuns left the order, which was a little unusual, whereas the rest of the nuns housed at the Abbey remained in the religious life.

Conversely, it is equally possible that the poor Abbess is actually completely innocent of the accusations levied, and they were just part of the scandalous moves by the King to rid himself of the yoke of Catholicism.

Whatever her actual fate, it is clear there would have been a great deal of scandal and shame attached to the events at the time, so either way it is perhaps no surprise that her ghost still wanders the scene of her crimes. According to one writer, she was still active in the second half of the 20th century as she was seen by a young couple lingering outside for a goodnight kiss.

November 1st

Great Hyde Hall, Sawbridgeworth, Hertfordshire

Great Hyde Hall was built in the late 1590s, and was a beautiful square building with extensive grounds and holdings. Although still a listed building, today it is divided into privately owned flats and apartments.

Our ghost concerns one of its previous owners from its glory days.

Sir John Jocelyn, son of the oddly named Sir Strange Jocelyn, died on November 1st 1741. He was a bachelor at age 52 (somewhat unusual for those days), and seemingly was very fond of his horse riding and hunting. He left instructions that on his death his favourite horse was to be slaughtered and buried with him. Since the nearby church refused to have any truck with such sacrilegious nonsense, his instructions were explicit that he was to be buried within the circle of yew trees on the driveway leading up to his ancestral home.

Although Sir John was in fact buried there, it is uncertain as to whether his wishes were ever carried out and his beloved horse laid to (early) rest beside him. Since then, on the anniversary of his death, it is said that you can see him riding his phantom horse up the driveway towards the property.

Some versions even go so far as to claim his horse is breathing fire. One presumes that if his wishes were not adhered to, that is what leads him to remain restless on the anniversary each year. There do not however seem to be records giving any indication that his spirit is still active now.

Cley Hill

See 15th March for the full entry.

Halstock, Dorset

A small village in Dorset, Halstock boasts the ghost of a saint.

The legend is that in the 7th Century, there was a pious young girl called Juthware, whose mother died in childbirth. Her father, Benna, tried to raise her alone but then remarried – finding himself a widow called Goneril to wed, who already had a son called Bana from her first marriage.

Eventually Benna died, and Goneril decided to rid herself of her unwanted stepdaughter. She devised a plan whereby she convinced her son that Juthware had secretly gotten herself pregnant, and had left the child to die in the woods to hide her lack of chastity. So incensed was Bana at Juthware's behaviour, that he drew his sword and beheaded his step sister there and then.

To their horror, the wrongfully accused corpse proceeded to pick up the severed head, and march itself Frankenstein fashion down to the nearby Church, where it reverently lay the severed head on the altar before losing its ghastly animation, collapsing in front of the altar, and moving no more.

Eventually, Juthware was canonised for her martyrdom, and became St Juthware. A local hostelry was probably named after her and was called The Quiet Woman.

However, ever since then, in a reasonably unsaintly fashion, her headless ghost is said to walk along the lane leading to the church. There do not seem to be any modern day sightings of St Juthware's ghost though.

November 3rd

Bruce Castle, Lordship Lane, Tottenham, London

Bruce Castle is an imposing building in Tottenham, now used as a museum and as the home of the archives for the London Borough of Haringey.

It is so named because originally, the land upon which it now stands and the holdings thereon belonged to the De Bruce family from Scotland – it was Robert de Bruce himself who gave up his lands in England.

When the 2nd Lord Coleraine, Henry Hare, inherited the property in 1667 on the death of his father, he renamed it to Bruce Castle and moved in with his young wife Constantia, the daughter of Sir Richard Lucy.

There seems to be some evidence that Henry was actually having an affair with Sarah Alston, who was married to the Duke of Somerset, John Seymour. It was reported (albeit some 200 years after the events) that his marriage to Constantia became increasingly strained, so much so that Henry confined her to the upper floors of the house so that he should not have to see her.

Allegedly, he eventually locked her in a small room beneath the tower, but she had access to the balcony from there and one night in November she chose to end her miserable existence by flinging herself and their young child to their deaths on the unforgiving ground below.

Since then, it is said that her wraith can be seen on the balcony and sometimes her forlorn cry as she falls is heard. Historically, it is known that Constantia died in 1680, but curiously her death is not recorded in the church records, even though they are present for that period. It's possible that this was because she *was* a suicide.

Henry went on to marry Sarah Alston, and then when she eventually passed away, he married a third wife, before finally passing away himself at the age of 72.

There do not seem to be any recent sightings of the ghost.

The Sun Inn, Saxilby, Lincolnshire

The tale of the haunting relating to this Inn is fascinating. It is said that one Tom Otter was employed in Saxilby in 1805, and started a dalliance with a young lady called Mary Kirkham.

When she became pregnant, he married her without telling her that he was actually already married. The night of the wedding, 3rd November 1805, he murdered her using a hedge stake, and when her body was discovered she was carried into the Sun Inn, along with the murder weapon. Tom was arrested and tried at The Sun, and then sentenced to hang.

Ever since then, it is said that on the anniversary of the murder there is an indelible bloodstain which appears in the pub, that the cries of Mary's baby can be heard, and the stake, no matter how strongly it is locked away, returns itself to the site of the murder.

The reality is that this version of the story, and the haunting, was first written in 1859 by Thomas Miller, and was only ever meant to be a piece of fiction based on some historical truth.

Like many urban myths, it has grown its own momentum and the haunting is now more often reported as exactly this. The actual historical truth is really the usual sad tale of infidelity, but ending in brutal murder.

Tom Otter was indeed working around Saxilby at this time – but he was working under the false name of Tom Temperell. (It is not recorded why he was using a false name at the time). He is described as being a malicious and revengeful man, who often maimed or injured the horses and donkeys he worked alongside in his job as a canal banker. He is also described as being stout and handsome, and this perhaps explains his apparent success with the ladies.

Tom was married to Martha Rawlinson in 1804, and they had a child together. She was not with him at Saxilby, having presumably remained at their home town of Eakring in Nottinghamshire while he went away to work, and so the locals at Saxilby did not know that he was married. He was courting Mary Kirkham at Saxilby, and eventually she of course fell pregnant.

At that time, the law stated that the Parish would have been responsible for the upkeep of any unwed mothers and their children – and would have to seek reimbursement from the fathers. Of course in reality, the fathers were rarely found or made to pay up if they disappeared – and so the practice of "knob-stick" weddings was commonplace – what we would think of today as a "shotgun wedding". The Parish councillors in this case did indeed intervene and forced Tom to wed Mary on 3rd November 1805 in the parish of South Hykeham – she was around 8 months pregnant at the time. Once he had wed her, whether he stayed or not, she was his responsibility to maintain financially.

The newly married couple were seen later that day a few miles away crossing Saxilby Bridge together, and the next morning, poor Mary's body was found, bludgeoned to death with a stout hedge pole that still lay close to her battered head.

Tom was arrested, and although the location is not specified, it is very likely that the inquest held was at the Sun Inn, since most Parish meetings were held there. As was the practice at that time, Tom was charged by the Coroner Mr Drury and twenty local residents with the murder of Mary, and then was sent to Lincoln for trial at the Lent Assizes. It is entirely likely that Mary's body would also have been carried to the Inn.

After Tom was charged, Mary was taken away and buried at St Botolphs Church in Saxilby.

Tom was duly found guilty of her murder on 12th March 1806, and was hanged, having first confessed his sin to the priest. Before being hanged, he was measured for the gibbet chains – and apparently this act finally broke his spirit and he went to the gallows a subdued and frightened man.

In those days, the law required that murderers should not be buried. Their bodies were "hung in chains" or "dissected" in order to avoid burial – and Tom's body was taken to Saxilby Moor, close to where he committed the crime, and hung from a gibbet post in a form fitting set of chains with a head collar, designed to keep the slowly rotting corpse and then skeleton intact for as long as possible to serve as a warning to others.

Gruesomely, it is reported that Tom's skeleton remained hanging there until strong winds blew down the gibbet pole some 44 years later. During that time, in 1832, the Magazine of Natural History reported that a pair of Tomtits had nested in the skeleton's open mouth, and successfully raised their brood from that dreadful perch.

This gave rise to a short poem being penned:

> "There were ten tongues all in one head
> The tenth went out to fetch some bread
> To feed the living in the dead"

After the gibbet eventually succumbed to the ravages of nature and fell, the rusty remains of the old head collar reportedly found their way to Doddington Hall and were kept there on display. Just to the south east of Saxilby, the B1190 is still called Tom Otters Lane, probably in remembrance of the gibbet.

Nevertheless, the stories of hauntings at the Sun Inn have persisted, and although the ghost tale written by Tom Miller can be dismissed as largely fictional – it does leave the possibility that some form of haunting is still present.

Certainly the pub was visited by the Bassetlaw Ghost Research Group accompanied by a BBC reporter in 2014, and they reported hearing loud noises, and the door twice banged in response to questions. They felt there were actually a number of ghosts present in the pub, and not just Tom, so it might be that any night of the year is likely to have paranormal activity. The pub itself was refurbished and re-opened in July 2017.

November 4th

Ardgillan Castle, Balbriggan, County Dublin

On November 4th, 1853, Lady Louisa Augusta Connolly, wife to Lord Langford and mother of four children, entered the sea just below Ardgillan Castle for her customary daily dip. She was staying at the castle with her friends whilst her husband was on a hunting trip in Scotland, and liked to make use of its proximity to the shoreline to take an invigorating short swim in the sea. There was a secluded little cove of rocks there which she liked to use, but being a rocky cove it also meant that there was quite a strong undertow in the waves there.

Lady Louisa went down to the sea for her dip just after midday, and remarked to her maidservant, Charlotte, that the water seemed a little rougher than it had the day before. Charlotte tried to persuade her mistress not to enter the water, but her ladyship was undeterred.

Charlotte informed the subsequent inquest that she quickly saw that Lady Connolly was struggling, and waded into the water to try and reach her – but was unable to get to her through the waves. She went back to shore and took off her outer layer of clothing and tried again, but to no avail. She then ran for help to some men working the fields nearby, but they would not enter the water as they said it was too dangerous and they could not swim. By this time they could see Lady Connolly lying on her back in the water and not moving.

Eventually, after Lady Louisa had already been in the water for nearly an hour, the gardener from the castle was brave enough to try and get to her, and he did manage to catch hold of her and start pushing her ahead of him towards the shore.

However the sea swell was too strong, and snatched her motionless body away from him once again, and he was forced to give up.

Finally at 1.40pm, a boat which had been launched to try and save her managed to bring the body ashore, but by then Louisa had drowned.

Ever since then, on the anniversary of her drowning, her ghost is said to walk from the beach up to the castle, walking up the steps now named Lady's Stairs after her. They say she is looking to see her four little children who were left without their mother at the tender ages of just one year old up to six years old. Sadly the children's father also died less than a year later, leaving them all orphaned.

Curiously, I found one source (repeated frequently in other sources but clearly all taken from the one root story) which claimed that the ghost was waiting for her husband who had drowned, and that she did so on Halloween – but either this is just a case of confusing the facts, or this is a very unlucky place to swim and there is a second story where it was the man who drowned.

November 10th

Melbury Bubb, Dorset

Melbury Bubb is a tiny hamlet nestled against the side of Bubdown Hill, which used to be a beacon hill in days gone by, when the only way of communicating quickly over long distances was by beacon fires lit on hilltops to form a line-of-sight warning system.

In 2013, the hamlet was estimated at having only 40 residents. The church there does have a significant oddity – the base of the font is clearly made from a recycled much earlier piece of stonework – perhaps a standing cross – since the carvings on it are all upside down!

According to one of the gravestones in the churchyard, one Thomas William Baker, a local farmer, was murdered at the age of 72 on 10th November 1694.

The story is told that robbers struck when he was driving his horse and cart along one of the lanes there on his way home from market, but the horse continued on home, thus alerting the family to search for him.

Ever since, his ghost has been still driving the horse and cart on its final journey down the quiet lane, which is now dubbed "murderer's lane".

Unfortunately, there is no real historical trail to follow this up.

There is certainly a grave memorial to "Thomas Baker, Alias Williams" in the churchyard at Melbury Bubb, and it tells us that he was in fact murdered on 10th November 1694. It doesn't give any details as to how. He was 74 years old.

The first record of the story of the ghostly horse and cart seems to come from a book by Roger Gutteridge in 2009, who quoted his source as the Dorset Yearbook from 1949.

A 90 year old witness was said to have recalled it from when she was 7 years old, which would have been back in 1865.

As far as I can find, that is the only recorded mention of it ever having been seen, which would tend to stretch the definition of "haunting every anniversary" to its absolute limit if it was only ever seen once in 400 years.

Frankly, it would also surely be quite surprising if a 74 year old back in the 1690s would actually be fit and strong enough to drive his wares to market alone?

Perhaps the tale has twisted over time, and the old farmer does still haunt the lane which he spent probably many peaceful hours of his life time quietly driving his horse and cart along.

November 11th

Haroldlea House or Thunderfield Castle, Horley, Surrey

This ghost story seems to relate to this general area – although some sources claim it happens in the doorway of Haroldslea House, and some at Thunderfield Castle. Most seem to plump for the general area of Haroldsea Drive.

The story goes that on 11th November every year, just after sundown, the sound of a tolling bell can be faintly heard, getting a little louder as the minutes pass. Shortly thereafter, a ghostly troop of men is said to march by – either through the doorway of the house, or along the road, or up to the castle, depending on which source you read. At least one source claims that they were men marching to fight with King Harold at the Battle of Hastings and they rested at the castle there before marching on (presumably) to their doom at the Battle of Hastings.

There are some real problems with each of these versions, so let's start with the most obvious. The Battle of Hastings was on 14th October. Even if you take into account the change of calendars since then, the men would not be marching around on November 11th.

More pertinently, there is absolutely no evidence that there was ever a castle here. There are the remains of two curiously ringed moats, and it is quite possible this was a fortified manor house, of the half-timbered type. It's possible there could have been a motte and bailey, but again there is no certain evidence for this.

Haroldsea House was built in 1859 – so again – the men weren't marching through that if they were from 1066. It was built on the site of an older building known as Harrowsley Manor Farm, so it's always possible that was named for the local manor at what later became known as Thunderfield.

There is still a Harrowsley Green Lane passing across the fields behind Haroldsea Drive, so clearly all the names are interconnected over time.

I have been unable to find any reports of actual sightings here – perhaps it is time someone conducted a vigil on the right night, somewhere near the site of Thunderfield. It's quite easy to spot on Google maps.

November 13th

Royal National Orthopaedic Hospital, Brockley Hill, Stanmore

This ghost must have the least detail to go with it of almost any ghost in this book. The story is that every 13th November a grey lady wanders through the wards – and there is some speculation that the hospital was built on the site of a nunnery.

No-one that I could find gives any comment as to who she is or why she haunts, or what the significance of the date is.

Even the renowned supernatural author Peter Underwood, writing about it in his book Haunted London, wryly remarked that he was once told by a nurse that every hospital she had ever worked in was apparently haunted by a grey lady.

November 19th

Somerleyton, Norfolk

There is a legend that a giant used to roam around Norfolk, causing havoc wherever he went.

His name was Grabador, and he would get up to all sorts of mischief. He was the brother to one of the Cornish Giants.

One day, he sat on a hillside idly watching a local lad digging a huge pit in the ground, and lining it with sharp stakes. After a while, he realised what the man was up to – he was building the same sort of device which had caught and killed several of the giant's Cornish brethren.

Furious, Grabador snatched the man up into the air, and crushed his body with his bare hands, so that the man's blood rained down on the ground.

Now every year on the anniversary of that event – spectral blood is said to rain down onto the fields around Somerleyton.

Perhaps unsurprisingly, I can't find any records of it actually ever being seen.

November 29th

Foulksrath Castle, Jenkinstown, County Kilkenny, Ireland

Foulksrath castle is actually a fortified tower house, and has been through various iterations and rebuildings since at least 1349 a.d. It spent quite some time as a youth hostel from around 1949 until 2009, but is currently privately owned.

There is a legend that one night a guard who was supposed to be on watch on the battlements fell asleep during the uncertain times following the English Civil War, when many lands previously held by families loyal to the crown were given away to men loyal to Cromwell.

Foulkrath in particular was given to one of Cromwell's own officers, a man named Bradshaw. The previous family were allowed to go on living on and working the land around the castle, and clearly that was a delicate situation which could flare up at any moment.

The lazy guard was discovered snoring by the master of the house, who was so incensed with rage at the dereliction of duty, that he flung the young guard over the battlements to his death.

On the anniversary every year, the guard's footsteps can be heard along the parapet and the sound of the door opening and closing as he tries to make amends and perform his duty as he should have done in life.

It was supposedly visited by a BBC crew in 1992 who claimed to have recorded some very clear sounds during their investigation. Ghost Circle also visited the site and reported some interesting results.

November 30th

Old Church Road, Romford, Essex

There is a legend that there used to be a church along here which sank into the ground. Since then, every November 30th, its bells can still be faintly heard.

Looking at how urban the area is now, I'd surprised to hear anything over the general hubbub of city life, and unsurprisingly I cannot find any actual records of anyone hearing the bells.

Curiously, Kirksanton in Cumbria has a virtually identical legend, but not tied to a specific date.

Chapter 12 – December

Bramber Castle, Bramber, West Sussex

Bramber castle was built as a Norman Motte and Bailey castle (a single tower built on a mound with a surrounding defensive ditch) by William De Braose who became the 1st Lord of Bramber. He was one of William the Conqueror's favourites and was granted extensive land in England for his part in the wars.

The legend is that William De Braose's children were seized by King John I after he angered the King, and were starved to death in Windsor Castle. Ever since then, their pitiful wraiths can be seen begging for food around their old home of Bramber Castle around the time of December each year.

Historically, though, this legend bears no truth.

It was actually William de Braose IV who was alive during the reign of King John, and he was married to Maude de Braose (nee Maude de St Valery) who was renowned for her beauty as well as her strength and wisdom. The two were believed to have had around 16 children, but historical records really only give us a clear picture of nine of them. Of those nine, all of them reached adulthood and either married or joined the clergy.

Maude was a favourite of the King's at court, but she fell from favour when she was somewhat sharp in her opinions about the death of the King's nephew, coupled with the fact that her husband William owed the King a sizeable sum of money. She tried to flee the King's wrath by escaping to Ireland with her eldest son William, but they were captured and imprisoned first in Windsor Castle and then later in Corfe Castle.

Maude (a lady in her middle fifties at this time) and her son William V (himself married with children) were indeed starved to death at either Corfe Castle or Windsor castle in 1210 a.d.

Neither of them could possibly be described as children of course. Maude's husband William IV died in exile in France, having been stripped of much of his title and wealth by the vengeful King. In fact, it was partly the shameful treatment of the Lady De Braose and her eldest son that led to the tight wording of the Magna Carta which King John was eventually forced to sign to remove some of the monarch's rights.

William V's four young sons were imprisoned alongside their father and grandmother, but they did not die, and were released from their captivity in 1218. At least one of them went on to claim back some of the land and title owed him following the King's perfidiousness.

It seems this tale is more legend than fact, wreathed around folk memory of a shocking act by a King towards his nobles. However, it doesn't mean that there aren't any ghost children at Bamber – just that they may be wrongly attributed. They could just be the ghosts of some poor beggar children who died one cruel winter.

There have been a number of ghost investigations at the site in recent years.

In 2002 on ghost hunting group captured a photograph which showed a strange inexplicable mist forming on it – even though the photo was taken in broad daylight and there was no mist that day. Sometimes these photos are actually the breath of the photographer – but in this particular shot that didn't seem to be the case.

Shoreham Ghost Hunters were there in 2009, and another team visiting in 2008 saw a hazy white light shining in the castle. Curiously a brother and sister ghost hunting team conducting a vigil in December 2014 also saw a strange light shining on the stone floor in front of them.

It does seem very possible that the site remains active – even if the tales that go with it have become a little skewed over time.

December 4th

Lewisham Station, London

At approximately 18.20pm on this fateful night in 1957, the electric train to Hayes, carrying approximately 1500 passengers, was held on a stop signal just outside Lewisham station under the bridge.

It was an exceptionally foggy evening, and the weather had been causing problems for hours, with trains running late and out of sequence, so the signalmen were diligently trying to ascertain which train they had got and where in order to get all the commuters home.

As the train waited at the red signal, it was hit from behind by a steam locomotive towing carriages with around 700 passengers on board. So violent was the collision that the impact collapsed the bridge down onto the first two carriages of the steam train. A third train which was about to cross the bridge overhead narrowly missed being part of the carnage when it managed to stop in time without plunging off the collapsed bridge.

Around 90 people died that day, and a farther 100 or so were hospitalised with serious injuries. The train lines were shut for days, whilst new track had to be laid and a temporary bridge installed. The "temporary" bridge is still in use today.

Curiously, one man recalls that his father, a man of habit, always caught that train every night to commute home from work – and never deviated from his routine, even if he had to run to make sure he got on that particular train. On this one night, he was running to catch it when for the first time ever, he suddenly thought "it's not important" and stopped – taking a more leisurely walk to get the next train. The sudden random change to his pattern probably saved his life.

In 1985, a railway inspector was waiting for his bus home at about 2am in the morning near the bridge where the disaster occurred, when he heard a voice crying out for help. He called the police when he could not locate the person, and when they arrived they could also hear the plaintive voice. However, they told the man not to worry about it – they were often called out to this spot and it was voices of the long dead victims of the rail crash that were still crying out – not any live person in actual danger.

It would be interesting to find out if these cries can still be heard.

December 19th

Wilsons of Haworth, Haworth, Yorkshire

This building is converted from an original row of three weaver's cottages, and spent 38 years as a restaurant called Weaver's restaurant before bung purchased in 2013 and renovated into the now charming Wilsons of Haworth Guest House.

There is a story that the ghost of Emily Bronte can be seen walking in its garden every year on this date. Emily died aged just 30 on 19th December 1848 of tuberculosis, just three months after the death of her brother, whom she loved dearly.

The whole family was generally malnourished and suffered from ill health (all six children and their mother pre-deceased their father) – and Emily was so thin at the time of her death that her coffin was only sixteen inches wide.

I have been unable to find any actual accounts from anyone who saw the ghost.

December 20th

White Horse Inn, Great Baddow, Essex

Great Baddow is now situated on the outskirts of Chelmsford. The White Horse Inn, now part of the Ember Inns chain, is a charming old white building fronting straight onto the street. It dates back to the 17th Century.

There is a legend that on 20th December one year, a group of farm workers went into the pub for a well-earned draught of ale after their toils. There they bumped into the crowd of bell ringers from the nearby St Marys Church.

As the ale flowed, the young men on both sides got a little rowdy, and eventually a drunken fight broke out. One of the farmworkers accidentally killed one of the bell ringers in the brawl, and immediately fled the scene. He escaped to the nearby church and ran up the tower, but there he caught his foot in a bell rope, tripped, and plunged to his death.

Ever since then, the sound of footsteps or cries on the stairs or near the toilets within the White Horse Inn is heard on the anniversary each year.

Sadly, I could not find any records of anyone actually hearing it. There is however supposed to be a second ghost – that of a traveller who was murdered here for his money bag and buried in the garden.

December 21st

Stiperstones, Shropshire

The Stiperstones are an unusual geological formation within the Shropshire Hills Area of Outstanding Natural Beauty. The unusual formations of the quartz stone ridge were formed during the last ice age, when they were high enough to poke out of the top of the encroaching glaciers, and be subjected to freezing and thawing and all the elements could throw at them in that harsh climate.

Today, the various formations have wonderful names such as Shepherd's Rock, Devil's Chair, and Cranberry Rock. One of the formations didn't do as well as its cousins in the naming game – and is stuck with the unimaginative but accurate moniker "The Rock".

There are all sorts of legends surrounding the Devil's Chair in particular, but for the Stiperstones in general the legend we are concerned with is that on the midwinter solstice, all the dead of England from the previous year meet here in order to pay homage to the King of the Damned.

The landscape itself is certainly very evocative in its unusual and majestic beauty, and has clearly had an influence on local belief systems and lore for a considerable length of time, since some Neolithic stone cairns have been identified up amongst the stones themselves.

Wycoller Hall, Colne, Lancashire

Little remains of Wycoller Hall today apart from some stone built ruins in the centre of what is now Wycoller Country Park. It was originally built in 1550 by Piers Hartley, but he died without a male heir. As a result, the Hall passed into the hands of his daughter Elisabeth, who had married a man called Nicholas Cunliffe.

The legend is that on this night in December each year the sound of a horseman frantically galloping up to the hall can be heard, where according to one version he brutally murders his wife for being unfaithful. In another version he chases a fox into the building, riding his horse right up the staircase and into the ladies chambers. His poor wife was so terrified by his snorting horse and sudden appearance that she became hysterical, and he was so angry at her cowardly display of histrionics that he threatened to strike her with his riding crop – at which threat she fell down dead from sheer fear. In most versions of the story, the gentleman in question is listed as Simon Cunliffe.

The historic difficulty with the story is that there is no record of a Simon Cunliffe. The estate passed on down through the hands of the eldest male of the Cunliffe family through four generations, but they tended to all be called either Nicholas, John, or Henry.

Finally, in the early 1700s Nicholas Cunliffe died without any heir, so the estate passed to his brother Henry. When Henry also died without an heir, the estate was passed down through their sister's family. Their sister had married an Owen, so her grandson Henry Owen inherited on the condition he took the name Henry Owen Cunliffe.

Henry took on the by now somewhat impoverished estate and lived his life spending far above his means. When he died in 1818 his nephew Charles should have inherited, but in reality the debts were so high that the hall had to be broken up and sold off to pay everyone they owed money to.

The full story of the horseman seems first to have appeared in 1873 in "Lancashire Legends" by John Hartland and T. T. Wilkinson. In this version, he is not named Simon, but is said to be just the transparent figure of a horseman who gallops up to the hall, dismounts and runs inside, whereupon a woman's screams are heard followed by unearthly groans. The transparent figure then runs back out, remounts and gallops off.

As far back as 1776, the hall was referred to as "the haunted hall" which would tend to suggest the ghost predates both the grandson Henry and his great-uncle Henry that he inherited it from.

Curiously, one ghost hunting team visiting in 1996 recorded "the sound of a riding crop".

December 21st

Pendeen Vau, Pendeen, Cornwall

Pendeen Vau is an ancient fogue, near the village of Pendeen in Cornwall. Today, it is sited practically in the farm yard of Pendeen Manor Farm. As such, it is not open to the public. A fogue is an underground, stone chamber built in either the Bronze or Iron Age, of which only 15 have been found in Cornwall, and some in Northern Europe and Orkney. Pendeen Vau is thought to be between two and three thousand years old.

In the early 1600's, John Norden wrote of it,
> "Pendene Vowe, a holl or deepe vaute in the grounde, whereinto the sea floweth at high water, very far under the earth: Manie have attempted, but none effected, the search of the depth of it"

The fogue is today known to be seventeen meters deep, and not close enough to the sea to have it rushing in – which leaves me wondering what they heard down there in the early 1600s that they associated with the sea at high tide.

There is a legend that a tall woman dressed in white can sometimes be seen at the entrance to the fogue. She turns and enters it if seen. Occasionally she is said to hold a red rose in her mouth, and some versions give her appearance as winter solstice, others as Christmas Eve. Some of the legends say that if you see her, your doom is sealed and you will die within the year.

A team of megalithic photographers calling themselves "The Rascals" visited the fogue and explored it in August 2001.

They took a great number of photographs and remarked that even though they spend a lot of their time crawling around in ancient underground tunnels and burial chambers, this one had a particularly uncomfortable feel about it which made them feel a little nervous and creeped out. All of their photos of one particular section of the wall kept showing up with a "fogged" dark cloud in them, which they were at a complete loss to explain.

Studland, Dorset

This is a curious little legend which seems to have sprung from a story told by Benjamin Pond in the Andover Advertiser in the 1960s. He stated that the events had actually happened in 1929.

A fisherman who worked along the coast and river here often had to walk home at odd hours of the night, depending on the tide and how far inland he could bring his boat. On this particular night, he became slightly spooked by something he could see ahead of him which seemed to be glowing white in the moonlight.

As he bravely drew nearer, he realised that he was only looking at an old donkey, whose white coat happened to be reflecting the moonlight as it grazed peacefully on the riverbank.

Thinking himself every kind of fool for allowing himself to be spooked, he went to walk past the beast – when to his horror it simply vanished right in front of his eyes.

He supposedly mentioned his stories to others in the locale, and was told that this apparition would appear every year on the same day (which also happens to be winter solstice). He was told that it commemorated the murder of a local farmer when years before who was ambushed and murdered whilst riding home on his white donkey.

Another version of the tale says that the donkey belonged to a fisherman who was attacked and then left unconscious to die of exposure by an escaping deserter from the Navy.

Whichever is the truth, there don't seem to be any other sightings of the donkey – so perhaps people are mistaking it for a live animal and paying no mind to it when they see it. Or perhaps the truth is just that it is what it is - a story.

December 23rd

Grafton Regis, Northamptonshire

The story goes that on 21st December, 1943 villagers at Grafton Regis were awoken during the night by the sounds of battle; men crying out, swords clashing and guns firing.

Another version of the tale says it was a group of six workmen who heard the sounds, but could see nothing to accompany them. They were hearing the 300 years old to the day replay of the Civil War battle held here.

Factually, during the English Civil War, the parliamentarian forces led by Major General Phillip Skippon trapped the Royalist force led by Sir John Digby at Grafton Regis Manor House. According to records, the Manor House held out for "about a week" before surrendering on Christmas day.

There don't seem to be any records of anyone ever hearing the ghostly sounds again, which makes this another rather dubious entry for an "anniversary" haunting. More pertinently, there don't seem to be any records of it being mentioned in the local papers at the time. On the one hand, this would perhaps not be surprising since the country was once again at war – albeit this time a World War with the battle fronts in other countries – so a ghost story may well not merit column space given the much more important things going on at the time.

On the other hand, if an entire village woke to what they thought were the sounds of a nearby battle, it might be supposed that *given* the fact a war was going on at the time, panic would ensue as they might believe the fighting had indeed reached our shores?

December 24th

Buckle up for the long haul for Christmas Eve: it is without a doubt the most popular night of the year for anniversary ghosts!

Hever Castle, Kent

Hever Castle is a stunning little gem of a castle situated in Kent, a little to the west of Tonbridge. It was originally built in 1270 a.d. but in 1460 passed into the ownership of one Henry Bullen. Like all ancient buildings, it has been added to and changed many times over the years, but some parts of its Tudor heritage still remain – and it is the Tudor times that interest us.

Henry Bullen's son inherited the castle, and it was he who changed the family name to Boleyn.

It seems quite likely, although not known for sure, that Anne Boleyn was born here. She certainly spent the majority of her youth here. Her older sister Mary, although herself already married, was having an affair with King Henry VIII, and so clearly the family had a good standing at the Royal Court.

Mary gave birth to a son, and caused the gossip to run rife when she named him Henry. Divorce was not yet a possibility at that time in our history, and maybe the King was not sure whether the boy was his or his mistress' husbands. Whatever the cause, his roaming eye fell on Anne next, but she was a bit more coy about allowing the King's advances.

The King pursued his new love interest quite devoutly, and his determination to have her as his wife caused the history of England to change forever as it was the catalyst for the rift between Crown and Church.

Anne and Henry were married in secret in January 1533, and he declared her his Queen in the summer of that year.
Her ending, as described elsewhere in this book, was tragic, and she is now often cited as being "the most travelled ghost" in England, since many locations around the country claim to have visits from her spirit.

Hever castle is no exception – claiming two cyclical visits from her in the month of December (see also Boxing Day, December 26th).

It is said that on Christmas Eve each year her ghost can be seen crossing the bridge over the River Eden in the castle grounds. Some versions say that she starts her walk from beneath the mighty oak tree in the gardens where she and Henry often courted, and other versions say she pauses on the bridge to throw a sprig of holly into the water.

Since The King and Anne were married in January, the romantic in me can't help but wonder if she chooses Christmas to haunt because that's when her lover finally proposed to her.

In 2007 the television programme Most Haunted investigated the site, and in 2008 the spoof video by Most Spooky Live was released on YouTube.

In 2012, one visitor reported that they had felt a presence in the Long Gallery, and in 2013 another visitor took a photograph outside the castle which clearly shows an orb in one of the doorways. Interestingly, although orbs are most notoriously produced by digital cameras because of the way they work, the photographer says this photo was taken with a 35mm camera.

In 2015 another visitor took a photograph which he believed showed the spectral hand of Anne Boleyn.

His photo, reproduced in several national newspapers at the time including the Daily Mail, shows a misty slightly elongated hand shape with its index finger pointing towards the fireplace.

Unfortunately, it also shows extreme blurring of every light source in the room – with a left to right movement and trail of light. The "hand" follows exactly the pattern of this movement trail, and is almost certainly just the trail left by the moving camera from some minor light source or lens glare.

Strata Florida Abbey, Near Tregaron, Wales

Strata Florida Abbey is listed by most sources as translating from the Latin as Vale of Flowers. It was founded in 1164 a.d. for the Cistercian monks, and suffered the same fate as many holy establishments during King Henry VIII's reign and the Dissolution of the monasteries. For a brief time during its later history, it is rumoured to have held the Holy Grail within its hallowed walls.

For many years after its downfall, it was said that on Christmas Eve a ghostly monk could be witnessed trying in vain to restore the ruined altar, and candles could be seen it within its walls at night. Some versions say it was always seen on Christmas Day.

In addition, there is a little legend too that at nearby Llyn Gwyn Lake, which traditionally supplied the Abbey with fish, a monk cursed the lake when King Henry VIII's soldiers came to tear down the walls, saying that the fish therein should forever bear witness to the horrors that were being perpetrated that day. Thereafter, the fish caught there would give forth a weird croaking sound whenever they were caught, to the point where none of the locals would eat from its stock anymore for fear of bringing bad luck down on their households.

I'm not aware of any sightings of anything paranormal in recent times. If you know of any – drop me a line.

Roos Hall, Beccles, Suffolk

Roos Hall is a red brick built building with a strange looking "crow stepped" gables. It is a Grade I listed Tudor Manor house dated 1583. Although privately owned, it can be viewed by prior arrangement.

It is said that every Christmas Eve a coach and horse rattles it way up the driveway to the main door. The horses are headless, as is the coachman, and sometimes a lady sits next to him. She must presumably have her head in place, since it is claimed that looking her in the eye can be a fatal experience.

One source I found speculated that the driver was thought to be a member of the Blennerhassett family, but other than that there seems to be no further detail to explain the reason for the haunting.

The Blennerhassetts were originally from Cumbria but came to Norfolk in 1423 when Ralph de Blenerhayset married a 14 year old rich heiress (and already herself a widow!). They therefore were owners of Roos Hall for a time, but why one of them should be haunting it on this particular day remains a mystery.

Rochester Castle, Kent

Rochester Castle, boasting the tallest castle keep in England, dates back to at least 1087 when the Bishop of Rochester commissioned its building. As with any British castle, it has a fascinating history and makes its second appearance in this book. This time, it is not for something which happened at the castle, but apparently simply for love of the old building.

Charles Dickens, one of the most well-known and celebrated writers in British history, was extremely fond of this monument, spending much time here during his lifetime. When he died, he apparently requested that his body be interred in the old Burial Ground on the site of the castle, but given his importance to the nation it was decided he should actually be buried at Westminster Cathedral. He died in 1870, and it is said that since then his ghost can be seen walking around the moat and the cemetery on Christmas Eve.

There seems to be no explanation as to why he should choose this particular date: his birthday was in February and he died in June, so there seems no outwardly obvious connection to the date, other than of course one of his most famous pieces of writing is a ghost story which takes place on Christmas Eve.

ASSAP (Association for the Scientific Study of Anomalous Phenomena) visited the site for an overnight vigil in July 1992 and recorded metallic clicks, heavy thumping sounds, and a light turning itself on and off when it should not have. Sheffield Paranormal visited in October 2009 and although they reported nothing specific they felt the site had potential for real activity.

Bomere Pool, Near Condover, Shropshire

More a legend than a ghost story, I include this one just for interest. Bomere Pool is a 25 acre area of water just a few miles south of Shrewsbury. It is actually, in geological terms, a "Kettle Hole Mere" which is a type of lake specifically formed by the retreating ice at the end of the last ice age.

It used to be fully open to the public, but for the last decade or two it has been privately owned and is used as a watersports centre. There is still a public right of access along the northern shore of the lake. In 1986, the bones of a woolly mammoth and three juvenile mammoths were found nearby.
There is evidence of an Iron Age settlement along the southern edge, and we know that there was once a large Roman settlement here.

The legend is that there used to be a prosperous settlement here (maybe the Roman one?), which was visited by a travelling priest who wanted to preach Christianity. He tried to build his church here, but the locals mocked him so much that they angered his deity – who caused the water to well up and sink the settlement, church and all. (It seems a shame to take the church too!)

Since then, on Christmas Eve, the church bells can be heard tolling sonorously underneath the water.

Madingley Hall, Madingley, Cambridgeshire

The Hall was originally built in 1543 by John Hynde, and remained in the same family for over three hundred years, being added to and modified along the way as such beautiful old buildings always are according to the fashions and fortunes of the times. It passed out of the family's hands in 1871, and after a couple of other private owners was eventually bought by University of Cambridge in 1948. Since then it has been used as a residential conference centre.

Our ghost is said to be that of John Hynde's wife, Ursula. John died in 1550, leaving his son Frances to carry on with the building of their magnificent hall. Frances is said to have ordered the closure of the nearby Histon church, and used the stone and timber as building materials. The contents of the church he sold off for revenue. His mother is said to have been distraught by his sacrilege, and the sorrow it caused her contributed to her decline and death.

Her ghost can be seen on Christmas Eve, walking the route between the Hall and its nearby church. She is reported to have been seen by a soldier billeted there during World War II, and also by an au pair from her small bedroom in the turret in 1951. Since the university took the building over three years prior to that alleged sighting, it's difficult to see what need a university would have had for an au pair, which brings the truth of that particular story into question.

The Naked Scientists conducted a ghost investigation on October 31st 2017 but sadly with no tangible results that they couldn't immediately debunk.

Sandringham House, Sandringham, Norfolk

Best known for being the residence for the Royal Family at Christmas each year, the estate at Sandringham is glorious for visitors, with 240 acres open to the public, as well as tours of the museum and parts of the house.

Every Christmas Eve, it is said that poltergeist activity within the building starts to ramp up, with cards being thrown about, lights turned on and off, books flung to the floor and bedcoverings pulled off. The maidservants start to travel in groups in certain parts of the building, afraid to go alone because of the heavy wheezing sound that is likely to follow them if they do.

Even Prince Charles is rumoured to have encountered an unpleasant sensation of being followed there, but unfortunately we will never get any full detail simply because it is after all, a Royal residence and therefore intensely private.

Stubley Old Hall, Rochdale, Derbyshire

The historical records of Stubley Old Hall are somewhat lacking in detail over some parts of the centuries, but it has been around since at least 1330 a.d. since there is a record of its sale then by Nicholas John de Stubley.

The legend here is that the Lady Fatima was due to be married to Ralph de Stobbeley. Depending on which version you read, either he went away on the Holy Crusades and found another lover abroad thus leaving poor Fatima bereft, or else she went with him on the crusade but died before they made it back to England.

Either way, he returned home, and took another bride, whom he married on Christmas Eve. However, the wedding was interrupted by the sound of a harp playing.

Ralph went outside to investigate, but when he didn't return the guests and his new bride went looking for him – only to find him lying dead with a look of sheer horror on his face.

Since then, the sound of Fatima playing her harp can often be heard on Christmas Eve.

The crusades were roughly speaking between 1095 and 1291 a.d., so that would place our characters (if they existed) firmly before Nicholas John de Stubley sold the property in 1330.

Today the property is privately owned, and there are no records that I can find of anyone hearing the harp play.

High Laver, Essex

Even today, High Laver is still a very small village, with around 500 inhabitants. Its main claim to fame is that the philosopher John Locke is buried there, having spent his last few years living in the household of Sir Frances Masham until he died in 1704.

Abigail, Baroness Masham is the subject of our ghost story here. She is said, once a year on Christmas Eve, to drive her coach past her old home of Otes Manor in High Laver and gaze at it longingly.

In historical record, she was said to be a plain woman, born Abigail Hill, who although of good birth fell on temporary hard times when her father ruined his branch of the family financially. She was lucky that her cousin Sarah raised her out of penury by finding her a place in the household of Queen Anne.

Much to Sarah's chagrin, over the ensuing years Abigail rose to the position of one of the Queen's favourites and closest confidantes – usurping the spot from Sarah herself. There were even rumours as to the exact nature of the relationship between the Queen and Abigail – but that is perhaps more down to the spiteful jealousies of court gossip.

Abigail married Samuel Masham, and it was through him that High Laver became her out-of-town residence.

After Queen Anne died, Abigail retired from court life and lived out her days at High Laver, dying on 6th December 1734 and being buried at the church there.

It's unclear exactly where the house was, but it seems likely it was about a mile west of the church at High Laver.
There don't seem to be any records of actual sightings of the ghostly carriage.

Kersal Cell, Salford, Lancashire

Kersal Cell is a 16th Century Grade II listed timber framed manor house, now situated in the busy suburbs of Salford. Originally it was built on the site of a former cluniac priory, which itself was built on the site of a hermit's cell – hence the name echoing down the ages today.

Some legends say the hermit was actually a local Knight – who went away to the Crusades but began to question whether all the killing was as righteous as he had originally thought – so decided to return home. Unfortunately, he found his wife dead and on her way to be buried when he got there, and so full of remorse was he that he retired to Kersal and became a hermit there.

Some of the timbers still in the house date back to 1515. As far as I can ascertain, it is currently privately owned, having spent part of its life as a pub and restaurant and then standing empty for some time.

The legend is that every Christmas Eve, a ghostly monk can be seen walking outside the house.

I have been unable to find any detail about why this should be the case, and the only record of any kind of sighting I could find unfortunately doesn't gave the day, only the year: 1959.

Supposedly, a policeman was walking his nightly beat with his police dog (an Alsatian) plodding faithfully at his side. He made his usual round, which included checking on the old hall.

All was well there, and he made his way up the path towards the road. As he did so, he clearly heard footsteps walking up behind him.

Turning, he could see nothing, but his dog became very agitated, crying and straining at the leash to escape. It need hardly be pointed out that this was extremely unusual behaviour for a Police dog. The footsteps continued towards them and on past, all the while with nothing to be seen.

A newspaper report from 1966 mentions the ghost of John Byron (a well-known poet and hymn writer associated with the house) being seen inside the house but at no particular time of year. It also mentions that part of an ancient tunnel had been found underneath the building, which at that time was being used as a country club. Curiously, it makes no mention whatsoever of the Christmas ghost – which beggars the speculation that this tale is actually a more modern construct.

Another newspaper clipping from 1971 details how an 800 year old stone fireplace had been found hidden behind one of the walls upstairs when the property was undergoing renovation.

In 1977 the Manchester Evening News ran an article on the ghosts of what was now a pub at Kersal Cell. It claimed that there was the ghost of a monk who had been walled up alive in the cellar for getting a local girl pregnant, and that the baby itself could also sometimes be heard crying. It also claimed there was some poltergeist type activity, with glasses being thrown, the sound of a bell ringing, and doors slamming. I might be sceptical, but the article was clearly trying to drum up trade since the landlord at the time was trying without success to get public funding to help with the cost of the upkeep of the ancient building. Historically, even when it was a priory, it looks likely that there was only ever one monk there – so it is highly improbable that he would have been walled up to die. It's quite possible that this is where the story of the monk's ghost springs from.

By the mid to late 1990s, the property had been sold off and become private dwellings – split into three homes according to one newspaper report and two according to another.

St Mary's Church, Worstead, Norfolk

St Mary's Church is said to be the haunt of a White Lady ghost who appears every Christmas Eve. So famous is the legend that even the pub next to the church renamed itself to "the White Lady".

Originally, the White Lady was said to be something to be terrified of, for to see her was to bring about certain death. The original story says that in the 1830's, a man scoffed at the tale of the ghost, and vowed to go in there on Christmas Eve and meet her. When he did not come out, his friends went in to find him, and there he was, cowering down in the belfry and mumbling "I've seen her". He died shortly afterwards.

The White Lady, however, has been seen as a more friendly presence since 1975, when Diane Berthelot and her husband were visiting the church, and he took a photo of his wife sitting on the pews.

It is today a very famous ghost photograph which can be found on literally dozens of intranet sites if you want to look at it and make your own mind up. Diane said that she had felt enveloped by a peaceful presence whilst she was there, and that she had not been feeling particularly well and was on antibiotics at the time. She felt better after their visit to the church, but it was only when the photographs were developed that they claim the figure behind her was noticed.

Every site seems to list it as a lady in white wearing old fashioned clothes and with a bonnet, and even though the photo was taken in summer, are keen to attribute it to the White Lady legend.

Personally, what I see in the photograph sitting behind Diane is an older lady wearing black slacks and a pale coloured top or jacket and white hat of the type my own grandmother used to sport in the 1970s. I'm pretty sure I can even make out her modern day footwear.

There is a shaft of bright sunlight falling across her, and it is lighting up her white top and white hat in the otherwise darker church into a sort of halo blurring effect. I can even make out where the shadow edge of the shaft of sunlight falls across the "ghost's" very solid looking leg. One of my friends has a photo of himself taken inside a dark ancient church standing in a shaft of sunlight – and he too looks like he is bathed in some kind of holy light. It is, however, just a trick of the camera trying to differentiate between the extreme light and shade.

The Bertheholts swear no-one else was sitting there that day – but in their own account they didn't notice the figure until much later, after the film was developed and they were showing their holiday snaps to some friends. Having spent many years as a fraud investigator, I am well aware of how unreliable the human memory is, and I think it is very likely they just didn't recall that for a brief moment, another perfectly human and solid visitor took a restful seat in the pew behind Diane. Still – take look for yourself and form your own opinion.

No Mans Land, Holford, Somerset

This is listed in most sources quoting the ghost story as "Normansland". The story is that at the stroke of midnight every Christmas Eve, a coach drawn by four black horses makes its way up Normansland driveway, circles round, and then disappears. Sometimes a female passenger can be seen on board.

The difficulty is in working out what would count as "the driveway" and quite what is meant by "Normansland".

There is no property called "Normansland" that I can find at Holford, but just to the south east of it is a large rugged area of land called No Man's Land. The main A39 runs alongside it and there are track-ways across it in places, so really the coach could be on any of these.

Blackgreve Farm, Hedley Heath, Wythall, West Midlands

There is a legend here that on Christmas Eve every year, you can hear the frantic screaming and neighing of dying horses.

Some versions of the story attribute the ghostly sound to a Roman chariot drawn by a pair of horses, which slipped on ice and tipped over into either the ditch, or the moat at Blackgreves farm. The two horses screamed and struggled but were drowned.

Other versions attribute the accident to a much later period coach and four, which careened out of control and into the moat. Again, the team of horses could not be rescued and were drowned.

Blackgreve farm has certainly been around since at least mid-1100's as there are records of its sale. It is a moated farm, and although the farmhouse which sits on the island formed by the moat today is of a later date – around 1870 – there would have been buildings here prior to that.

I am sceptical of the Roman version of the tale, since the Archaeological Watching Brief carried out in August 2015 firmly places all finds as no earlier than medieval, and moated farmhouses of that period were a common construct in this area. The Romans would have left nearly a thousand years earlier. But since the brief also confirms that the moat was around 12 to 17 metres across, there would certainly be possibility for a cart or coach to turn over into it and drown the horses.

The property is privately owned, and there do not seem to be any reports of recent encounters of the spectral noise.

Oak Hill Park, East Barnet, London

The curious legend here is that the ghost of Geoffrey De Mandeville rides through Oak Hill Park, across to the nearby catholic church, where he disappears through the wall. What makes it unusual, is that he supposedly only does this once every six years, on Christmas Eve.

Geoffrey was a Baron, and from the sounds of it quite a ruthlessly self-serving man. Queen Matilda and King Stephen were busy arguing out who the rightful claimant to the throne of England actually was – and Geoffrey cheerfully swapped sides between them every time one of them offered him some more land and title.

Eventually King Stephen gained the upper hand and became more than a little peeved at Geoffrey's perfidiousness. He stripped him of some of his land and title, and had him excommunicated from the church for desecrating holy grounds. He had to tread a little carefully in not completely defeating and ruining the Baron in case it set the other noblemen even more on edge than they already were.

Geoffrey was killed during a skirmish in 1144. He died quite a slow death, and perhaps had time to become afraid of what excommunication meant for his immortal soul. One history says the Knights Templar took his body to their church, where they had his coffin suspended from tree above the graveyard – so that although technically not in holy ground, he was at least in a holy enclave.

Quite what the significance of the six year interval is, nor of Christmas Eve, no-one seems to comment. Geoffrey died in September, so there is no obvious connection there. He was last due to make an appearance in 2016, but there seems to be no mention of anyone in the area getting startled by a man on horseback when they returned from their Christmas Eve partying.

Egremont, Cumbria

There is very little detail at all on this ghost – and nothing of any recent sightings. Supposedly, many years ago, a farmer went missing when he went to ride home on Christmas Eve after making merry with his companions at the local inn. He was never seen again and his body never found. Since then, he can sometimes be seen wending his way around the lanes around Egremont on his faithful horse on Christmas Eve.

Travellers Rest, Brough, Derbyshire

The Travellers rest is still a picturesque pub and inn today, and with six ensuite bedrooms you could spend quite a comfortable Christmas Eve waiting for this ghost to appear if you chose.

Most versions say that the ghost that appears is that of a young farm wench, who was in the pub one Christmas Eve and tried to escape the grasping hands of some rowdy revellers by running down to the cellar. Unfortunately she tripped and fell, and the fall killed her.

Another version is that she was actually a traveller whose coach was forced by an encroaching snow storm to stop there one Christmas Eve in the early 1800s whilst she was on her way to visit relatives. As she went to make her way up the stairs to her assigned bedchamber, one of the drunken patrons tried to pull her down on to his lap. She was horrified at his forward behaviour she broke free and ran up the narrow staircase – but missed her footing near the top and fell. Her neck was broken in the fall.

It's particularly curious that the two versions refer not only to different people but to a different staircase: one being the stair to the cellar the other being the stair up to the bedchambers. Whoever she ism, the ghost is also supposed to make an appearance at other times of the year, and apparently one American tourist saw her in 1985.

Cross Keys Hotel. High Street, Saffron Walden, Essex

The Cross Keys Hotel is a fabulous looking half-timbered building that underwent an extensive renovation in 2012. Said to be 850 years old and dating back to Elizabethan times, it sports a ghost every Christmas Eve.
According to some sources it is the sound of a man running down one of its passages or sometimes the sight of him as well. Other sources say it is the sound of marching, and attribute the haunting to a Cromwellian soldier.

At least one ghost hunting team has conducted an overnight vigil there, but they did not publish any tangible results.

Kempston Manor, Kempston, Bedfordshire

The Kempston Manor which stands today was built fairly recently – in 1815. The story goes that one Christmas Eve, the Lord and Lady of the Manor had gone out to a Christmas Ball. Returning home by coach and horses at a late hour, they were devastated when their young son, who had waited up to see his parents come home, dashed out to greet them but got tangled in the horses legs and was crushed. He died of his injuries, and now every Christmas Eve the sound of coach wheels and a child screaming can be heard.

The original manor at Kempston was there at least as early as 1254 a.d, since there was record of it being sold. It seems likely that it was a substantial and wealthy manor with extensive holdings at that time, but as the centuries passed it declined in status until eventually it was only being used as a home for second sons who would not inherit a main estate, or dowager aunties and the like who needed a modest home of their own.

It was in considerable disrepair and partial disuse by the time it was torn down and rebuilt in 1815. Celebrating Christmas the way we think of it in Christmas cards – ladies in bright dresses and wearing fur mufflers stepping through the snow into the waiting carriage to go to balls or deliver presents – really only started in the late 1700s, early 1800s. Since it seems that the old manor was half dilapidated and mainly occupied by dowager aunts prior to being torn down and replaced in 1815, it seems unlikely this tale dates back to before then.

But there are no records that I can find since then of a child of the owners being killed, so it is always possible that the tale is much older but has become embellished over the years.

There do not seem to have been any recent records of the grisly sounds being heard.

Whitwell, Hertfordshire

There are several villages called Whitwell around the country, but we are interested in the one in Hertfordshire, not far from Hitchin and the sprawling town of Stevenage.

Legend says that there is the ghostly sound of an axe chopping wood, and then a tree felling, which can be heard on Christmas Eve on the lane from Codicote to Whitwell in Hertfordshire. The sound is supposed to repeat all through the night.

Some sources cite the lane as being Bendish Lane in Whitwell (which is definitely not the lane towards Codicote). Certainly, there used to be a pub in the village called The Woodman which was apparently named after this ancient ghost story.

There is also a tale that two real life woodsmen were frightened half to death when their colleagues dressed up in white sheets and clanking chains and leapt out on them where they were working one night in the woods along Bendish Lane in the middle of the 19th Century.

This later tale suggests that the ghost tale is therefore much older – since the pranksters were using it to scare their poor mates, who apparently never did figure out they had been pranked but spoke for the rest of their lives of the night they encountered the ghost of the woodsman.

Welwyn, Hertfordshire

Not very far from Whitwell lies the very attractive small old town of Welwyn (not to be confused with the much more recent and bigger Welwyn Garden City).

One of the houses on the hill leading out of the main high street still bears an old metal sign affixed to its wall asking coach drivers to slacken the bearing rein on their horses to allow them to put their weight into pulling the coach up the hill.

A bearing rein was a piece of harness which forced a horse to hold its head in a proud arched shape: but which actually was incredibly painful for the hours after long hours spent in harness with a cricked neck, and also forced the horse to breathe unnaturally when trying to pull a coach. Many a fine, expensive carriage horse was ruined because its "wind was broken" – a term to describe horses who could no longer breathe properly. Anna Sewell, who wrote "Black Beauty" was instrumental in having these signs put up in order to try and save the cruelty to horses.

One source I found claims that every Christmas Eve the ghost of an elderly gentleman wanders the High St, knocking on doors. There seems to be no reason why that I could find, and no records of any actual sightings.

Bradgate Park, Leicestershire

Bradgate Park in Leicestershire is 800 acres of enclosed deer park – and contains the ruins of Bradgate House. Still open to the public today, it has wonderful woodland walks and a couple of tearooms – so well worth the visit.

Bradgate was the birth place of Lady Jane Grey, bequeathed the throne of England after King Edward VI's death, and who was Queen of England for just nine days in 1553 before being beheaded in February 1554 on a charge of treason whilst still only a mere 16 years old.

Bradgate House fell into disuse after 1739, and was in ruins by 1739.
The story is that on Christmas Eve Lady Jane Grey gets into her carriage at the house and rides down to the local church, where she and the carriage disappear. Some versions say the carriage actually rides towards the house, not away from it, and that the horses pulling it are headless.

Ghost walks are quite regularly held by the Park, which the public can attend.

One set of ghost hunters in December 2013 filmed what looks very like a figure walking beside the ruins of the house. You can watch the video on Youtube and see what you think – look under "Ghost of Lady Jane Grey at her home in Bradgate".

Dunkenhalgh Hotel and Spa, Clayton Le Moors, Lancashire

Dunkenhalgh Hotel, as it is now, is a 700 year old manor house – complete with turrets. There has certainly been a manor of some sort on the site since at least 1285, when it first appeared in recorded history – but it is undoubtedly much older than that.

The tale goes that the family who owned the manor, the Petres, hired a young French governess called Lucette to teach their children. Lucette unfortunately fell in love with a young officer who came to visit the family, and was foolish enough to let him have his wicked way with her. He rode off promising to return for her, but of course he never did, and she suddenly found herself in an extremely compromising position which simply would not be tolerated by the household when they found out. Lucette dare not either stay, nor try to go home to France – for her shame would soon become glaringly obvious to all.

She would pace about the grounds trying to think of her way out of her dilemma, and hoping against hope to see her suitor return and make an honest woman of her. Eventually, she realised she was waiting in vain, and despairing for her future and that of her unborn baby, she flung herself to her death in the river from the bridge in the grounds.

Her ghost is still said to haunt the scene every Christmas Eve, and appears wandering by the bridge wearing her grave shroud.

Another version of the tale gives her name as Lycette, and says it was the head of the household, Captain Starkie, with whom she fell in love.

A number of guests over the years have claimed to see a woman – and one guest took photos at a wedding he was attending there. The photos were taken in broad daylight of the bridal party out on the lawns of the property. Later, when the family were enjoying looking at the photos of the happy occasion, his young granddaughter looked at one particular photograph and asked who the lady holding the baby was over by the trees.

Some other visitors camping near to the hotel one December were sure they saw a figure on horseback ride away from the hotel in the night.

Another person working at the Dunkenhalgh once saw the figure of a woman wearing white – and she looked as if she was laughing – but in total, eerie silence.

One ghost investigator who stayed there in 2009 recorded his findings, which included sounds of tapping, on YouTube.
It seems quite likely that this is an active haunting to this day.

Bradley Woods, Bradley, Lincolnshire

This is quite an ancient tale, which was possibly originally thought up to keep poachers out of the woods.
It is said that during the Barons War (1264) or possibly the War of the Roses (1455 onwards), a young woodsman lived in the woods with his pretty young wife and their baby son.

The husband was called away to fight in the war, leaving her struggling alone with a baby. She would wait by the edge of the woods every day hoping to see him returning home, but one day instead a group of three soldiers found her, and they sexually assaulted her. They then left her there on the ground, but snatched her baby son as they rode off.

She was left to wander the woods alone, bereft of both her husband and son.

She has apparently been seen many times over the years – either standing at the edge of the wood or walking through it – and is sometimes seen to run out in front of cars, whose poor drivers stop thinking they have hit someone real, only to find no evidence whatsoever of a real person.

Curiously one writer claims that this father was driving down Bradley Road one night and saw some leaves "walking" across the road – as if stuck to the bottom of someone's shoes – except no-one was there.

It seems the paranormal activity in and around the woods is still fully active – whatever the original cause.

Holy Trinity Church, Ingham, Norfolk

This beautiful old church, making its second appearance in this almanac, has some parts still remaining dating back to the 13th century, but most of the building was rebuilt in the 14th century and of course has gone through many changes since then. Up until the dissolution of the monasteries under King Henry VIII, it served as a priory, and it is probably from that period in its history that our ghost tale springs.

It is said that on Christmas Eve each year, the ghost of a monk wearing a white habit marked with the insignia of Saint Victor is seen wandering around where the ruins of the priory once were. He is joined by three other monks, and they make their way to the altar before disappearing.

I cannot find any records of actual sightings of these figures.

The Shipwright's Arms, Kent

The Shipwright's Arms is an ancient pub, first licensed in 1738, which stands on the banks of the Faversham Creek. It is an atmospheric building in an equally atmospheric location, and so it is perhaps not surprising that it boasts a Christmas ghost story of its own.

The tale is that one landlord many years ago locked his doors after the last of his happy patrons left on Christmas Eve. He tidied up his bar, and made sure everything was secure and ready for the next day before retiring to his bed. He had not been in bed long when he heard someone pounding on the front door of the pub.

Not willingly to rouse himself from his snug and warm bed on this cold and bitter winters night, he shouted out that the pub was closed for the night and he wasn't getting up to re-open for "man nor devil".

The following morning, he was horrified beyond reason when he opened the door and discovered a snow-shrouded corpse, frozen stiff, lying just outside.

Every Christmas Eve since then, the sounds of pounding, accompanied by gradually-weakening cries for help, are heard at the isolated old pub.

I could not find any records of anyone actually hearing the ghostly sounds.

Prospect Inn, The Quay, Exeter, Devon

Some versions of this tale give the date as Christmas day, but the landlord of the pub, speaking in 2015, stated it was Christmas Eve that the ghost manifests.

Prospect Inn is an attractive white washed building with lovely riverside views, and in the early 1800s was called the Fountain Inn. It changed its name in 1957, when the role of Manager for it was given away as a prize in a national newspaper competition. It was given a grand reopening by the well-known Diana Dors to celebrate the winners of the competition and its new landlady and landlord.

According to tradition, every year the ghost of a young girl (some versions say "little girl" others say "teenager") appears, dressed in Victorian style clothing and carrying a rag doll. She will smile sweetly at any one who sees her, but then promptly disappears.

Strangely, some versions of the tale say that some witnesses have found something slightly chilling and eerie about the knowing way in which she smiles.

One fairly recent set of visitors to the pub snapped a photo of themselves enjoying their night out, but one of the photos shows a strange, slightly head shaped blur showing behind the right shoulder of one of the party.

December 25th

Garricks Head pub, Bath, Somerset

This pub, situated so conveniently close to the theatre, boasts the ghost of an actress from the late 1800s.

Apparently the young lady took her last curtain call at the Theatre Royal wearing a striking grey dress covered in feathers which had been her costume for the play. She then returned to her rooms at the Garricks Head and committed suicide – because she had just found out that her husband had discovered her own extra-marital affair and had murdered her lover in a fit of jealousy.

She can still be seen every Christmas time either inside the pub or walking up to it from the direction of the theatre.

One worker recollects one of the tills in the pub suddenly launching itself four feet across the room, just as the staff were clearing up after closing time. Given how heavy the item was, this should have been impossible.

Cadogan Hotel, Sloane Street, London

Originally built in 1887, this impressive red brick building with Edwardian charm actually closed its doors in 2014 to undergo a full refit and refurbishment. Originally scheduled to reopen in 2017, it currently looks set to open its doors again in 2018 as the Belmond Cadogan.

The legend is that Lillie Langtry – the famously beautiful young actress who was one of the mistresses of King Edward II and who lived here for a while – still haunts the building on Christmas day each year. Apparently she only gets "felt" if the hotel is fairly quiet, and this is usually in the restaurant area. I was unable to find any actual sightings or tales of her, so it may well be this is more of an urban myth than actuality.

Coutts Bank, The Strand, London

Coutts Bank is a private banking service still used by the Royal family today.

Its impressive building on The Strand in London was said to house a number of ghosts and even a poltergeist. In particular around Christmas each year, the sound of children's happy laughter rings around the building. Most versions of the tale say this harks back to the time the building was frequented by toy sellers.

In 1993 the services of a medium were called upon and a service held to try and lay the ghosts to rest. Although specifically aimed to end the poltergeist activity it is possible it ended the Christmas manifestation as well as there seems to be little in the way of reports of actual witness sightings.

St John the Baptist Church, Boughton Green, Northamptonshire

Now just a set of crumbling ruins, this old church is still well worth a visit for its very charged atmosphere. There is still a natural spring which bubbles up under a low stone arch and which is thought to be a holy site.

It is said that around Christmas time, the figure of a beautiful woman is sometimes seen here and that if she asks for a kiss, you will likely die within a month. Also here are the ghosts of a local highwayman known as Captain Slash, and the sound of children's laughter is said to sometimes echo amongst the stones.

In 2016 we visited the site in broad daylight in summer and as we sat in the car just about to get out and explore, the clear sound of children laughing rang through the air for a few seconds – even though the church ruins sit utterly alone and no-one else was around.

Once we got out, we found the atmosphere very curious within the bounds of the church property, causing goose bumps to raise and the hairs to literally stand up on our arms. One of our dogs – a highly active young Belgian Malinois with utterly boundless energy – twice stopped his rambunctious play amongst the brambles and nettles of the overgrown parts of the churchyard and suddenly sat down facing away from us and about 30 yards away – leaning his head upward as if someone was petting him. Although I took numerous photographs, unfortunately nothing showed up in any of them.

Coincidentally, in June of the same year Indico Paranormal visited the site and recorded some interaction through their use of an Echovox (a device purportedly used to allow spirits to communicate via radio waves).

It would seem this site is still highly active even today.

Verdley Castle, Fernhall, Sussex

Verdley Castle is today little more than some rubble and an overgrown mound, hard to find within the woods that flank the small village of Fernhall in Sussex. Thought to have originally been a hunting lodge, it certainly dated back to at least the 13th century, but had fallen out of use and into ruin by the mid-1500s. In 1780 one Samuel Grimm made an ink wash drawing of it, showing a basic single rectangular footprint to the building, with just a few scant remains of walls still standing.

The legend is that the very last bear alive in the wild in England was hunted here and killed – and that ever since on Christmas day its spirit can be seen wandering the woods around the ruins of the "castle".

One television crew from Australia came and did quite an extensive investigation of the area, but alas found no trace of the bear. This was perhaps because they weren't filming on Christmas day!

In 2010 the film crew for the popular UK T.V. programme "Most Haunted" also visited, with little results again.

Strata Florida Abbey

See the entry for Christmas Eve.

Buckingham Palace, London

Before ever the Palace was conceived of and built, there allegedly used to be a monastery on the site. Supposedly, one of its inhabitants was punished for some long-forgotten deed, and still appears on the rear terrace at Buckingham palace every Christmas, heralded by the clanking sounds his chains make as he walks.

Unsurprisingly, for a Royal Palace, very little further detail other than the legend is recorded, since staff there are likely to stay properly tight lipped about what they may or may not see whilst going about their duties.

December 26th

Hever Castle, Kent

Ann Boleyn supposedly makes her second annual visit to her childhood home every Boxing Day, when her ghost can sometimes be seen or heard sitting in a small alcove off the Long Gallery, quietly singing in a sad sounding voice.

I have not been able to find any actual sightings of her.

December 28th

Tay Bridge Scotland

On this day in 1879, a steam train pulling six passenger carriages was crossing the Tay Bridge at 7.45pm. A violent storm of Gale Force 10 was raging, and had presumably damaged the structure of the bridge, since as the weight of the train passed over, the bridge horrifyingly collapsed, plunging the locomotive and all the carriages into the icy waters of the inky black River Tay below.

All 75 passengers and all of the crew were killed in the disaster. There was absolutely no hope of anyone surviving the terrifying plunge into the river as the bridge and train broke apart.

It is said that even today, the screams of the passengers can be heard on the wind on the anniversary of the tragedy, and sometimes the outline of a ghostly train can be seen still rushing along to its doom where the tracks once lay.

The bridge had only been open and in use for about nineteen months at the time of the disaster.

In 2012 a team called Haunted Scotland held a vigil at the anniversary time and date, setting up camcorders, digital cameras, and digital recorders in the hopes of catching evidence of the haunting. They quickly realised that it is possible to actually hear voices from nearby Dundee because of the way sound carries, and the current rail track also provides the back note sound of passing trains. They speculated that the forlorn cries of seagulls can also be mistaken for the sounds of a human voice. They did not capture any signs of paranormal activity, and felt it likely that any haunting has likely diminished over time.

December 29th

Lapford, Devon

Lapford is a small village of less than a thousand inhabitants. Sir Thomas a Beckett was brutally murdered on 29th December 1170 in Canterbury Cathedral in Kent, yet his spirit is said to haunt this small village many miles away. He can be seen galloping through the village on a white horse on the anniversary of his death: purportedly because one of his murderers came from around here.

I have not been able to find any actual sightings of this particular ghost – so it seems very likely it is just a myth given its very tenuous link to this historic tragedy.

St Mary's Church, Kemsing, Kent

Also related to the anniversary of the murder of Sir Thomas a Beckett, this small church claims that the figure of a knight visits the church every year and kneels briefly in prayer at the altar before disappearing. He is said to be the ghost of one of the murderers.

Some versions of the tale say he can be seen galloping up to the church on his horse before entering to pray.
As with the previous legend there seem to be no records of actual sightings, which tends to make this very likely also just a myth.

December 31st

Bramall Hall, Bramall, Manchester

Bramall Hall is a truly magnificent looking black and white Tudor mansion.

Run by the local council today as a visitor attraction and museum, it could also be used as a wedding venue – but you might want to avoid New Year's Eve as the chosen date for your nuptials.

Parts of the current building date back to the 1300s, but it was certainly a rich residence long before then since it is mentioned in the Doomsday Book.

The story is that one New Year's Eve in the 1630's, a rider clad all in red appeared at the hall and was given hospitality in the form of food and shelter. The next morning he had disappeared, but the owner of the hall, William Davenport, lay dead on the floor.

Since then, the ghostly rider visits on the anniversary of what is presumed to be his murderous deed.

If the date was right – it would put the deed in the time of the fifth William Davenport of Bramall, but since his son did not inherit until 1639, it seems likely that the fifth William died in that year. The fifth William would have been in his seventies at his death, and died at Bramall Hall according to historical records – but the manner of his death is not given.

Interestingly his wife Dorothy is recorded as dying in the same year – which does make me wonder if the story of the red rider is a euphemism for fever or disease, which perhaps carried off the elderly couple.

I could not find any records of actual sightings of the ghostly rider.

Lordscairnie Castle, Moonzie, Fife, Scotland

Lordscairnie Castle is actually the remains a moated medieval tower house.

What remains of the structure now was probably built in the middle 15th century, although an archaeological exploration in 2000 showed that the site had actually been occupied since prehistoric times right through the early and then late medieval periods – and there had been other buildings on site before the tower was constructed. There was at some stage a moat, but all traces of this have now disappeared.

The legend is that every New Year's Eve, you can see Alexander Lindsay, the 4th Earl of Crawford playing cards here with none other than Satan himself.

Quite why he should fancy a game of cards with the devil, no-one seems to know – and no-one seems to have recorded actually seeing him.

Overwater Hotel, Cumbria

For the full story, see New Year's Day at the start of this book.

Penselwood, Wiltshire

Penselwood is a small village in the historic county of Wiltshire. This ghost is said to haunt along the ancient track which runs between here and Stourton and which all sources I could find lists as "the Sloane Track".

The story is that on New Year's Eve one year a foolhardy local bet his companions that he could make the ride from Penselwood to Stourton in seven minutes. He cut across country, crossing the Sloane Track, but his horse stumbled and threw him – killing him.

Since then, his figure on horseback can be seen vainly trying to complete his ill-fated ride, still followed by his faithful dog. I can't find any record of The Sloane Track or see it on maps – so it's difficult to say where exactly this ghost might be seen.

There is a curious roughly ring shaped track-like feature showing on Google maps though – perhaps someone local could enlighten me as to what that is!

Runwell Hall, Wickford, Essex

Runwell Hall used to be a lovely double gabled manor house in the town of Wickford, Essex. In 1985 it became the Thomas Kemble pub, but is now the Toby Carvery, Runwell.

If you book your New Year's Eve meal there, watch out for a spectral carriage and horses driving up to the building, where the ghost of a lady is said to dismount. Her reasons and identity do not seem to be known.

There do not seem to be any actual sightings listed that I can find.

Peel Road and Bibby's Lane, Bootle, Lancashire

Now a residential area of mostly terraced housing in the heart of Bootle, this lane is said to be the location for the once yearly promenade of John Bibby in his coach. He is said to drive down the lane in his coach and four horses with his head in his lap. I can imagine that might put quite a dampener on people's celebrations.

Some versions of the story claim that he is on horseback, and headless.

Historically, John Bibby was born in 1775 and became an extremely wealthy shipping magnate: owning the company called Bibby Line. On the evening of July 17th 1840 he was walking home late at night, when something happened to him.

His body was found the next morning in a pond in Stand Park, about three miles from his home, which was close to where Bibby's Lane is now. He seemed battered and bruised, and there was a cut on his face. His gold pocket watch was missing – even though they dredged the pond to look for it.

The case was never solved despite a substantial reward being offered by the family. Opinion at the time was divided as to whether he sustained his injuries when he fell into the pond, losing his watch in the process, or whether he was mugged and his body rolled into the pond to hide it. Either way, there do not seem to be any records of actual sightings.

Purse Caundle Manor, Purse Caundle, Dorset

See the full entry on Midsummer's Eve.

Loch of Skene, Near Kirkton, Aberdeenshire, Scotland

This fairly small (as Lochs go) freshwater lowland Loch is the home of a somewhat strange haunting.

It is said that in the late 1600s, the local Laird (Lord) was Alexander Skene. He was known locally as "the Wizard" and it was believed he had travelled to Italy to practise a rare form of dark magic. It was also believed that he was in league with the devil.

One particularly cold winter's night, the Loch froze over (as it still does to this day). Alexander instructed his coachman to drive him and a mysterious passenger across the Loch in his coach. The coachman was instructed not to try and look at the passenger, but in the best tradition of all tales, of course he did look.

He realised it was the devil accompanying the Laird, and in his horror he lost control of the coach and team, and all plunged to their deaths through the breaking ice. All except the Laird and his companion; they apparently mysteriously survived. In some versions of the tale, all died, except of course Satan who flew away in the form of a black raven.

It is said that today, if the Loch freezes over, mysterious shapes in the ice can be seen – that bear an uncanny resemblance to the tracks of coach wheels. Every New Year's Eve, the coach can be seen drifting silently across the Loch before disappearing. Again, there do not seem to be any records of actual sightings.

Hockley Railway Station, Kent

There is a story that on New Year's Eve, one night in the 1960's, a young girl committed suicide by throwing herself off the bridge at Hockley Station, because she found out that her boyfriend was cheating on her.

Since then, the ghost of a girl crying her eyes out can be seen running up to the bridge on New Year's Eve.

Unfortunately for the tale, I can't find any record of a suicide at this station, nor of anyone actually seeing the ghost.

Ranworth Old Hall, Near Woodbastwick, Norfolk

The property known as Ranworth Old Hall dates back to at least the Doomsday Book. What was left of the old structure was finally demolished in 1985 leaving only what used to be the porch standing. In summer 2014, even this was damaged when an illegal rave (outdoors party) was held on the site.

Supposedly one Colonel Thomas Sydney lived at Ranworth Old Hall. He was an unpopular man, known to be a vicious drunk with a bad temper. On the area's annual New Year's Eve Hunt, he challenged his neighbour to a horse race.

Seeing that his neighbour was winning, he shot the other man's horse out from under him in full gallop – causing horse and rider to fall and breaking the rider's neck in the process.

The Colonel still attended the Hunt Ball that evening, showing no remorse or shame for what he had done. Suddenly, a hooded stranger entered the hall, swept up the Colonel, and exited. The Colonel was never seen alive again, but every New Year's Eve his ghostly form is seen struggling, laid over a horse's back with the devil riding.

Although one source claims to trace the story as far back as 1901, most sources seem to be quoting it from our old friend Charles Sampson and his book Ghosts of the Norfolk Broads – which have already proven to be more fanciful than fact.

There seem to be no historical records of either the colonel, or of any actual ghost sightings.

Knighton Gorges Manor, Isle of Wight

Making its third and final appearance in this book, the old manor of Knighton Gorges is supposed to make its annual reappearance either this night, or on New Year's Day (see January 1st.)

The tale is that one visitor was passing on New Year's Eve in the rain, and seeing people dancing inside the lit up hall in Regency costume, he assumed a New Year's Eve ball was in progress and hoped to find help and shelter from the awful weather there.

Unfortunately, despite his best efforts, no-one would answer his increasingly frantic knocks on the door, so he was eventually forced to give up and carry on.

He made his way to nearby Newchurch, and found help and a bed for the night. In the morning, his sceptical hosts took him to the site of the manor house he had seen the night before – and showed him that nothing but two stone pillars remained of the once fine manor house that had stood there.

Regularly visited by ghost hunters, it is claimed that even today electrical equipment will fail on the site with annoying predictability.

Interestingly, one source claims that the Isle of Wight has the most ghosts per hectare of anywhere in the world!

St Bartholomews Church, Arborfield, Berkshire

Arborfield is a very picturesque village in Berkshire, with the church occupying a site with a very pretty rural aspect and still hosting a very active congregation.

It is said that the ghost of a young girl visits the graveyard every New Year's Eve and stands forlornly beneath one of the Yew trees. She was due to marry a gardener at the nearby Manor, but was murdered by another suitor – the jealous butler. (I am bravely refraining from writing – "the butler did it" here…)

Unfortunately, there seems to be very little detail about to whom, when or why exactly this happened, and why New Year's Eve was significant – and even less about anyone actually seeing the ghost.

East Wellow, Hampshire

This is actually one village of Wellow in Hampshire, which is so spread out geographically that people refer to parts of it as East Wellow and West Wellow.

The Church of St Margaret is on Hackleys Lane in East Wellow, and is the burial place of Florence Nightingale.

A few short miles away lies the old manor house (now a school) of Embley Park, which was the birthplace of Florence. It is said that every New Year's Eve, a spectral coach and horses leaves Embley Park and dashes wildly towards the church.

I have not been able to find any records of actual sightings, nor any specific link to Florence Nightingale, who was neither born nor died around this time of year.

Molesworth Arms Hotel, Wadebridge, Cornwall

Yet another phantom coach and horses making its round on New Year's Eve is this one in Wadebridge. (The ghostly farriers must be quite busy this time of year, making sure everybody is ready for their annual jaunts out!)

The Molesworth Arms is quite spectacular looking with stone walls and timbered ceilings, and beautiful hanging baskets. Originally, it was a coaching inn, and now every New Year's Eve one of its former visitors makes his presence again, driving the coach into the inn. Supposedly people claim to have either seen it or heard the sound of it – but I can find no actual witness accounts.

Dower House, Fawsley, Northamptonshire

The Dower House in Northamptonshire is now just ruins – but very picturesque ones. Built in 1520 as a Hunting lodge for nearby Fawsley Hall, it went out of use by the 1700s and has stood slowly decaying ever since.

In 2014 it was in such danger of complete decay that a restoration project was begun.

The legend is that a huntsman – or at least a figure dressed in green - will appear every New Year's Eve and if seen either the viewer or someone close to them will shortly die. Quite what the history behind the legend is seems very unclear.

One ghost hunter caught a picture in 2012 which he believed showed a full bodied apparition at the site, which tends to suggest that there is still active paranormal occurrences there.

East Riddlesdon Hall, Keighley, West Yorkshire

This wonderful old building is currently owned by the National Trust and is open to the public.
The foundations here go back at least as far as 973 a.d. and the current ruins are at least 400 years old and were the home of a cloth merchant.

The tale is that on this night each year, a cradle kept in the main chamber will rock of its own accord. There are many other spirits also said to haunt the site all year round, but unfortunately overnight ghost hunts are not permitted. That being said, the TV programme Most Haunted did air an episode of their investigation of this site in August 2006.

In 2016 ghost hunter Mark Vernon believes he caught one of the ghosts on camera in the form of a misty shapeless mass which showed up in some frames and not others.

And finally...

If you have enjoyed reading this book (or not!), please feel free to leave a review on Amazon – it helps other people find it in the search engine. You can also find my first book on that same site if you type in my name – **Ghosts of Marston Vale**

But most importantly, please write to me with your own experiences at:

wa-1400@outlook.com

or visit my Facebook Page:

Ruth Roper Wylde

for details of upcoming projects etc.

My next book will be on hauntings along the roads and byways of Britain – let me know if you have seen anything whilst out and about .

Bibliography

2003-2011 Abbey Ghost Hunters
Accrington Observer
Ardgillancastle.ie
Bostonstandard.co.uk
Britishfolklore.com
Community.visitsscotland.com
Country Folklore Volume VI
Essexghosthunters.co.uk
Eerieplace.com
Ghostradio.wordpress
ghost-sightings.blogspot.co.uk
Haunted-britain.com
Hauntedearthghostvideos.blogspot.co.uk
Hauntingsofengland.com
Hauntedplymouth.blogspot.co.uk
Hiddenea.com
Inghamvilllage.co.uk
Kent News
Look and Learn Issue 740 20th March 1976
Lukeyardley.wordpress.com
Manchester Evening News
Mysterial.org.uk
Newsblaze.com
Occultandparanormal.webs.com
Spookyghost.wordpress.com
Threeriversrace.org.uk
UKmythology@wordpress.com
YouTube

www.avonparanormalteam.co.uk
www.bbc.co.uk
www.berkshirehistory.com
www.british-history.ac.uk
www.chilling-tales.com
www.cornwalls.co.uk
www.exetermemories.co,uk

www.explore-gower.co.uk
www.theguardian.com
www.heritage.norfolk.gov.uk
www.imnghamvillage.co.uk
www.kersalflats.co.uk
www.liverpoolecho.co.uk
www.londonghosttour.com
www.megalithics.com
www.mysteriousbritain.co.uk
www.mysterymag.com
www.overwaterhall.co.uk
www.paranormaldatabase.com
www.paranormalengland.co.uk
www.realorotherside.co.uk
www.rodcollins.com
www.saxilbyhistory.org
www.spookyisles.com
www.spottedghosts.com
www.scotiana.com
www.strangedayz.com
www.thenakedscientists.com
www.the-pigs.co.uk
www.urbanghostsmedia.com
www.walksoflondon.co.uk
www.whitbyuncovered
www.yourghoststories.com

Paul Adams – *Haunted St Albans*
Neil Arnold – *Haunted Bromley*
Geoffrey Ashe – *The landscape of King Arthur*
Gay Baldwin – *Ghosts of Knighton Gorges*
Jay Bartlett – *Exploring the unknown – the strange and the supernatural*
D.J. Bott *The Murder of St Wistan*
Daniel Codd - *Paranormal Lancashire*
William A Dutt – *Highways and byways of East Anglia*
David Farrant – *Dark Journey / Ghosts of Nettley Abbey*
Robin Gwyndaf – *Chwedlau Gwerin Cymru*
Anthony Hippisley Coxe – *Haunted Britain*
Alan Hughes – *Kingston Connections – the Story of Tainfield*

Peter Jeffrey – *East Anglian Legends and Lore*
Richard Jones – *Haunted Castles of Britain and Ireland*
Robert Kirkup – *Ghosts of the Northeast*
Clive Kristen – *Ghost Trails of Northumberland and Durham*
Theresa Lewis – *Spooky Wiltshire*
Harriet Martineau – *A complete guide to the English Lakes*
John Mason – *Haunted Heritage*
Rupert Matthews – *Little Book of the Paranormal*
Richard McKenzie – *They Still Serve: a complete guide to the military ghosts of Britain*
Frank Meeres – *Paranormal Norfolk*
Diane Mellmoyle – *Ambroth – Cumbria's Most Haunted*
Greg Morgan – *The Mystery of Knighton Gorges*
Tony Northwood *Icknield Way News 2005*
Roy Palmer – *The Folklore of Warwickshire (1976)*
Redditch Local History Society – *Lost but not forgotten – Moons Moat*
J F Rowbotham – *The History of Rossall School*
Charles Sampson – *Ghosts of the Broads*
Christina Schumacher and Ron Bowers – *A gift from spirit – Land of the wee folk*
Cavan Scott – *This Spectred Isle*
Jacqueline Simpson and Jennifer Westwood – *The Penguin book of ghosts: Haunted England*
Will Swales – *The Talbot Hotel – A brief history*
Elisabeth Thomas – *Haunted Hertfordshire*
Peter Underwood – *Haunted Farnham / Where the Ghosts Walk: the gazetteer of Haunted Britain*
John West Media blog
Jennifer Westwood - *Haunted England*
Diz White – *Haunted Cotswolds*
Alan Wood – *Military Ghosts*
Richard Young – *Whitwell's Notorious Seven*

Printed in Poland
by Amazon Fulfillment
Poland Sp. z o.o., Wrocław